CW00530535

COMMANDER CRABB
WHAT REALLY HAPPENED?

by John Bevan

COPYRIGHT © 2014 Submex Limited. All rights reserved.
www.submex.co.uk   e: books@submex.co.uk

No part of this book may be reproduced, stored in a retrieval system, or
transmitted in any form or by any means, electronic, electrostatic, magnetic tape,
mechanical, photocopying, recording or otherwise, without permission from the
Publisher.

British Library Cataloguing in Publication Data.
A catalogue record for this book is available from the British Library.

Printed by Everbest Printing Co Ltd
Block C Unit 5. 10th Floor 7 Ko Fai Road, Yau Tong Kowloon, Hong Kong
www.everbest.com

ISBN 978 0 9508242 7 7

This account is dedicated to the memory of
Cdr Lionel Crabb OBE GM RNVR(S) Retd,
a hero of the Royal Navy, whose outstanding
reputation has been suppressed for too long
to save "distress or embarrassment"
to those who were responsible for
sending him on the diving operation which
resulted in his death nearly 60 years ago.

CONTENTS

PART 1

Introduction

Preface

There is nothing more certain to give rise to damaging speculation than to impose a 100-year embargo on disclosure of the truth.

The public interest in Commander Crabb's disappearance continues to be an enduring mystery. It has only been intensified by the unusual decision to extend the security classification to 100 years (until 2057). The partially disclosed declassified documents state that the reasons for the extension are:

1. "exceptionally sensitive ... disclosure of which would be contrary to the public interest on security grounds;"
2. "containing information supplied in confidence, disclosure of which would ... constitute a breach of faith" and
3. "disclosure ... could cause distress or embarrassment to living personnel ..."

The extension has encouraged the growth and popularisation of conspiracy theories that are arguably even more damaging and embarrassing to the authorities and "living personnel" than the truth itself. The subject of Cdr Crabb's disappearance has even found itself on the official curriculum of at least one school.

Can the continued secrecy be seriously justified? Is it not now in the public interest to lift the veil of secrecy?

Perhaps it is time to re-examine the issues and put the above reasons for the continued embargo to the test.

There is a growing body of opinion that believes it would now be in the public interest for all the remaining classified information and documents to be released into the public domain, not least as a mark of respect to the memory of this WW2 hero who gave his life for his country; something that seems to have been overlooked as the bungled cover-up has unrolled, and rolls on with gathering momentum. Nobody the author has ever met, either in the services or civilian, has disagreed with this premise. Indeed everybody the author knows (and knew) who actually knew Cdr Crabb personally, consider it a travesty of justice that his story has not been told and his deeds for his country have not only failed to be fully recognised, but continue to be actively suppressed.

The following account is based on the best information available at the time of writing which includes documents released by the National Archives under the Freedom of Information Act in October 2006, published books, in particular *The Final Dive* by Don Hale (2007) and a personal investigation. The author gratefully acknowledges these sources of the information used in this book. But it has to be admitted that much of the information is hearsay.

The author welcomes any feedback, correction and constructive criticism of this account. Email: *info@drjohnbevan.com*

Background

Lt Cdr Crabb received his George Medal in 1944 for "gallantry and undaunted devotion to duty" during his hazardous diving operations in clearing mines from ships anchored off Gibraltar. He received his OBE for further hazardous diving operations which he undertook in Leghorn (Livorno) and Venice, Italy in 1945. In addition to these two medals for gallantry he was awarded three campaign medals: the 1939-45 Star, the Atlantic Star, the Italian Star plus the Defence Medal 1939-45 and War Medal 1939-1945 (Appendix 5).

Lt Lionel Crabb pictured in Gibraltar c1943 whilst in charge of the Underwater Working Party

Lt Cdr Crabb's medals
Left to right: OBE, George Medal, 1939-45 Star, the Atlantic Star, Italian Star,
Defence Medal 1939-45 and War Medal 1939-1945.

This distinguished war record would have seemed unlikely in a man who was just five feet five inches tall, a feeble swimmer, only able to swim about 90m (100 yards) without fins. He once confided in a friend that if he ever lost his fins he would drown. Furthermore, he had a healthy dislike for physical exercise and matters technical. When he had first applied to join the RN Reserve he had been turned down because he was then too old (28 years old), he was colour-blind and had a weakness in his left eye.

By 1949 Crabb was a retired Lt Cdr (Sp) but he was still on the RN Volunteer Reserve List (II). That year he joined the Admiralty Research Laboratory (ARL) at Teddington as a civilian contract employee where he worked alongside Lt "Jimmy" Hodges. Their principal activity was developing underwater film camera equipment and techniques and they produced two well-received films called "Report from the Sea Bed" and "Wonders of the Deep".

In 1950, Lt Cdr Crabb and Lt Hodges were called in to attempt to film the sunken submarine *Truculent* in the Thames estuary. A late

Left: Lt "Jimmy" Hodges (on ladder) with Dr Hans Hass in the Caribbean. Hodges died shortly after this photograph was taken.

Below: Cdr Crabb (*smoking*) and Lt Cdr Hodges (*right*) resting after their dive to the wreck of HM Submarine *Truculent* in the Thames estuary in 1950. On the left, bending down is Jim Hutchison. Cdr Crabb is wearing his two-piece dry suit whilst Lt Cdr Hodges is using a RN dry suit.

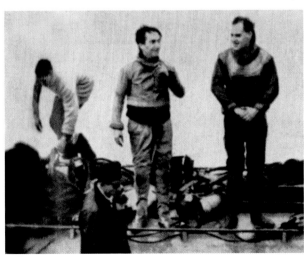

friend Jim Hutchison, then a diver in the RN, assisted them in the diving operation.

It is a sad coincidence that both Lt Cdr Crabb and Lt Hodges were destined to die diving, and both whilst using oxygen rebreathing equipment. Lt Cdr Jimmy Hodges died in 1954 whilst filming with Dr Hans Hass in Bonaire in the West Indies, as a result of going too deep whilst breathing oxygen.

In April 1951 Lt Cdr Crabb was involved in the search for the lost submarine *Affray*. He was the liaison officer between two ARL scientists and the deep diving team onboard HMS *Reclaim*. ARL had developed the world's first underwater television camera which successfully identified the submarine. One of the divers was the late Lt Cdr Bill Filer, an old friend of Cdr Crabb's.

On 12 October 1951, Lt Cdr Crabb was recalled into the RN with the substantive rank of Lieutenant Commander. The Admiralty placed him in the Countermeasures Group of the Underwater Countermeasures & Weapons Establishment, an outpost of HMS *Vernon* in Havant (UCWE; see Appendix 1) under the Commanding Officer of the Experimental Clearance Diving Team, Lt Cdr Gordon Gutteridge OBE.

From 1951 to 1956, Cdr Crabb had maintained a one-room apartment "off and on" across the road from Harrods at 2A Hans Road, Knightsbridge, London, SW3. The manageress was Amy Thomas who looked after a number of service flatlets at that address. He also had a private caravan which he kept for a while in HMS *Vernon*, a most unusual arrangement.

On 15 March 1952 Cdr Crabb married Margaret Elaine "Willie" Player. For a period whilst at UCWE, he lived with his new wife in his caravan in the grounds of Leigh Park House near Havant. This was the main administrative centre of UCWE, about a mile north of West Leigh House where most of the operational research and development took place.

Above: Margaret "Willie" Player who married Cdr Crabb in March 1952.

Right: 2A Hans Road, Knightsbridge where Cdr Crabb kept a one-room apartment.

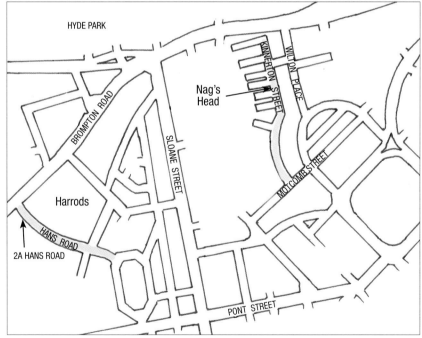

Map indicating the locations of Hans Road and the Nag's Head public house in Kinnerton Street.

The marriage failed and they split up in April 1953. She began proceedings for divorce against him and obtained a decree. He did not defend the proceedings and the Decree was made Absolute about December 1954.

Ron Chamberlain, a manager at Siebe Gorman & Co Ltd reminisced about Cdr Crabb:

"When he was in the Navy, he used to come to Siebe Gormans with the RN experimental team, to use our pressure pot[1] - so I got to know him pretty well. Boy could he drink, he used to go down to the Toby Jug at Tolworth, have three or four pints, then do a pot dive (where he couldn't get out, until the dive was over), the water level in the Pot certainly rised [sic]."

On 30 June 1952 Lt Cdr Crabb was promoted to Commander and put in charge of the UCWE Experimental Clearance Diving Team of seven Clearance Divers. However, in practice, Gutteridge continued to be in charge. Gutteridge described Cdr Crabb as not a natural manager and:

"… quite remarkably untechnical. Electrical circuits were a lifelong mystery to him, mechanical complexity was a bore, tools were for others to use … who hated scientists and innovation with a passion … his assessment of experimental equipment and techniques bordered on the bizarre … he was an elderly, unfit, near alcoholic chap … prone to propping up bars, heavy smoker and given to post-prandial naps."

He was retired from the position and the Royal Navy in April 1955 and was replaced by Lt Mark Terrell, much to the relief of Lt Cdr Gutteridge.

Meanwhile at HMS *Vernon*, Portsmouth, Lt Cdr Bill Filer was appointed the Officer in Charge of the Acceptance Trials Team for "self-contained diving equipment and other equipment used

---

[1] 'Pot' is a colloquial term for a compression chamber

Above: Lt Cdr Gordon Gutteridge OBE, c 1955. Pictured at the Royal Naval Physiological Laboratory, Alverstoke with his Experimental diving team.
Left to right, back row: Cdr Crabb, Jack Eaton (RNPL), unidentified, Lt Cdr Gutteridge.
Front row: Petty Officer Ron McKinley CGM and two unidentified divers.

Left: Lt Cdr Mark Terrell MBE who took over the Experimental Diving Team at UCWE from Cdr Crabb.

11

by CDs". The team was drawn from the Clearance Diving (CD) Instructors Staff at the Admiralty Experimental Diving Unit in HMS *Vernon* in 1954. Later, Filer was sent to Scotland as a diving instructor and Lt Cdr Joe Brooks took over the Acceptance Trials Team.

On 8 April 1955 Cdr Crabb was released once more from Active Service but he was again kept on the RN Volunteer Reserve list. He went on to work for an antique furniture dealer named Maitland Pendock in London who himself had a mystical reputation and died under mysterious circumstances (see Appendix 2).

Lt Cdr "Bill" Filer the Officer in charge of the Acceptance Trials Team.

On 11 October 1955, Cdr Crabb bought a two-piece dry-suit from C E Heinke & Co Ltd in Bermondsey, London. It is understandable why he preferred this suit as it would fit his short body better than the standard issue RN dry suit. Unusually, he had requested a suit with a neck seal as opposed to the standard, hood-attached version which he did not like.

Later the same month, Cdr Crabb and Stoker Sydney Knowles were commissioned by MI6 to carry out a covert investigation of the Russian cruiser *Sverdlov* whilst it visited Portsmouth at the Queen's Coronation Review.

The mission was successful and they discovered that the ship had a retractable bow thruster. He was paid £60 for the operation (this conflicts with Sydney Knowles who has stated Cdr Crabb received £2,000

Stoker Sydney Knowles BEM, long-serving diving partner of Cdr Crabb

whilst he received £1,000). Cdr Crabb had previously asked several colleagues, including Gutteridge and Terrell, if they would help him on the dive but they had both turned down the invitation. Prior to the investigation, Cdr Crabb had borrowed an old Italian oxygen set from the Experimental Diving Team and he tested the equipment by diving in Horsea Lake at Horsea Island. It has been said that he preferred this set to any other.

Cdr Crabb's *Sverdlov* project had been instigated by SIS (Secret Intelligence Service)/MI6 and unknowingly duplicated an investigation by a Royal Navy diving team working for Naval Intelligence Division (NID). This was a wasteful use of resources, an error which was to be repeated the following year.

In October of the previous year, around the same time that the *Sverdlov* was visiting Portsmouth, several HM ships visited Leningrad in Russia as part of an exchange visit arrangement. The Russians reciprocated by directing intensive intelligence probes, including the use of divers to examine the undersides of the British ships.

By this time, Cdr Crabb who was now 46 years old, had acquired a distinctive character. Gutteridge described him as:

"… a diver of enormous experience with a singular ability to endure discomfort, but not given to long, hard slogs underwater. His lack of fear was unquestioned … quintessentially curmudgeonly but kindly bantam cock, complete with swordstick with a silver engraved crab on the knob …

13

with his friends a most pleasant and lively individual … Small, dapper, given to velvet trousers, smoking jacket, spats, cane, monocle, extreme right wing and Royalist views and diffident, a staccato, rather wry way of speaking … lazy, not prone to making physical effort."

Cdr Crabb was in debt to the tune of £2,000–3000. This included arrears of alimony and his divorce case costs. He had no known assets apart from a share in the anticipated royalties from his biography being written by his friend Marshall Pugh. He told Harry Wardle that at one time he got a job as a model for a jock strap manufacturer. When Knowles paid him a visit on one of his regular trips to London as a lorry driver, he found Cdr Crabb on the street carrying a sandwich board. He was in a depressed state and became tearful when they discussed his menial situation.

PART 2

The Diving Operations

What were the objectives of the underwater investigations?

One year later, in April 1956, Soviet Premier Nikita Khrushchev and Marshall Nikolai Bulganin and paid a diplomatic visit to Britain at the invitation of the Prime Minister, Sir Anthony Eden. It was at the height of the Cold War.

They were brought to Britain in the Soviet cruiser *Ordzhonikidze* which was accompanied by two destroyers, the *Sovershenny* and the *Smotryashchie*. The Admiralty was very interested in several underwater

The Russian vessels that brought Kruschev to Britain in 1956.
The *Ordzhonikidze*, accompanied by the *Sovershenny* and the *Smotryashchie*.

features and characteristics of the cruiser *Ordzhonikidze*. Both MI6 and Naval Intelligence Division (NID) were eligible departments to gather such information. In the event, Cdr Crabb was commissioned by MI6 to carry out an investigation, whilst Naval Intelligence Division, not knowing about the MI6 operation, commissioned an independent investigation by naval divers.

The MI6/Crabb project to survey the Russian cruiser *Ordzhonikidze* in 1956 was run by Nicholas Elliott, MI6's London Station Chief assisted by John Henry his Technical Officer. Elliott has stated:

"... he [Crabb] begged to be allowed to do the job for patriotic as well as personal motives. There was no discussion of finance."

Elliott's involvement was perhaps unfortunate because he was a staunch friend and supporter of Kim Philby who was later to be unmasked as a Soviet agent and who defected to Russia. It is quite possible that details of the Cdr Crabb diving operation were leaked to Russia via this route, or even via Blunt.

Peter Wright in MI5 stated the Cdr Crabb project *"was a typical piece of MI6 adventurism, ill-conceived and badly executed"*. He added that Cdr Crabb was *"overweight and overage"*.

John Henry had stated, *"I told Nicholas not to use Buster; he was heading for a heart attack as it was."*

There are slightly differing versions of the objectives of the investigations.

According to Peter Wright of MI5 (author of *Spycatcher*) MI6 wanted to measure the propeller because of confusion in the Admiralty as to why she was able to travel so much faster than had been originally estimated by Naval Intelligence. Nicholas Elliott, head of the MI6 naval outstation in London, and who employed Cdr Crabb for the mission, stated:

"The navy were anxious to find out, as a matter of high intelligence priority, about certain equipment under the stern of the ship."

John Henry said the navy had been pressing him for months for details of the *Ordzhonikidze's* propellers. Chapman Pincher, an investigative journalist (author of *Treachery* and a friend of Peter Wright) also said Cdr Crabb was to investigate the propellers and rudder. This included measuring the pitch of the propeller blades. In particular, he claimed that Cdr Crabb was to check to see if the ship was fitted with a device code-named "Agouti" which was thought to reduce cavitation noise from the propellers. Another claim suggested he was to look for anti-sonar equipment and any mine-laying hatches.

The most credible version comes from Sir Edward Bridges, the Head of the Civil Service, who was commissioned by the Prime Minister to investigate the Cdr Crabb affair. He stated that Cdr Crabb's *"operating instructions were to restrict himself to an examination of the rudder and screws of the Russian cruiser."* He further explained that:

"Since December, 1954, one of the outstanding intelligence requirements notified [word obscured] *by the Admiralty has been information about the underwater noise characteristics of Russian warships. Indeed, this comes first in the list of Admiralty requirements since information is necessary for the effective use of certain types of mine and torpedo."*

When someone asked why Cdr Crabb had been employed, the answer was given, *"that he was especially qualified in tests of the kind in question".* And when asked why the test could not be carried out by HMS *Vernon*, the reply was that *"Vernon was not concerned with this type of test."*

However, recently released information indicates that the Prime Minister had initially sanctioned the following intelligence gathering operations against the Soviet ships:

1. Photographic reconnaissance and noise listening by aircraft.
2. Magnetic signatures by means of a D.S. loop (a Degaussing[2] System) at the entrance to Portsmouth Harbour.

---

[2] Degaussing is the process of decreasing or eliminating a remnant magnetic field.

3. 'Y' coverage (a magnetic characteristic of a ship)

4. Photographic operations whilst in Portsmouth Harbour.

None of the above involved the use of divers. However, two underwater operations had been proposed to Viscount Cilcennin, the First Lord of the Admiralty.

One was codenamed "CATAMARAN" and involved attaching a mechanism called a "catamaran" to the armour plating below the waterline. Possible objectives of this device have been suggested as being to measure the thickness of the armour plating ultrasonically and/or to detect any possible radioactivity which would indicate the presence of atomic weapons onboard. The latter would be consistent with a reference to the Soviet ships being "safe or unsafe" (see p.52).

The second was codenamed "CLARET". This included photographic and electronic noise listening by aircraft whilst the ships were at sea and does not appear to have included any diving operation.

But the Prime Minister, Sir Anthony Eden, ruled out any action that involved the remotest risk of detection and anything that involved attaching gadgets to the ships, including gadgets which would even just touch the ships. The situation was summarised by Admiral Sir Charles Lambe, the Second Sea Lord in a note to the First Lord on 6 June 1956:

> ... the only two operations proposed which involved service personnel were (1) that involving armour plate and a catamaran and (2) CLARET. Application for clearance for these two operations was therefore made to the 1st Lord. (1) was turned down by 1st Lord and (2) by the Prime Minister and both commented to the effect that nothing of the sort was to be carried out on that occasion. This comment was interpreted as applying to those operations (of the first type) for which the Admiralty was responsible. No such operation was conducted.

So both operations Claret and Catamaran were officially cancelled. But the directives did not specifically rule out any diving operations at all, depending on one's interpretation of "nothing of this sort". So it appears that both the Crabb/MI6 and RN/Naval Intelligence dives went ahead on the premise that they were just basic visual inspections.

Further clues as to the reasons for the survey came from a letter to the Prime Minister, dated 27 March 1981, which appears to be from Lt Cdr Joe Brooks:

"I was in charge of the Naval operational team who successfully surveyed the undersides of the Russian ships at the time to ensure that all was either 'safe' or 'unsafe'. The security services, apart from alerting us as to the need for this underwater survey operation, engaged Crabbe [sic] on a separate mission which failed disastrously."

The separate, naval diving operation is discussed below. The proposed and later cancelled Catamaran project, being an Admiralty inspired project, was more than likely intended as part of the Naval investigation and not the Crabb/MI6 activity.

The detailed objectives and achievements of the underwater investigations of the Crabb/MI6 and RN/Naval Intelligence dives appear to have been slightly different and they have not yet been clearly identified or disclosed.

Various theories concerning Cdr Crabb's disappearance

On the morning of Thursday, 19 April 1956, Cdr Crabb dived from a launch tied up at the South Railway Jetty just around the corner from three Soviet warships. He failed to return from the dive. The Admiralty and MI6 attempted to cover up the disastrous venture but botched it up. The cover-up thus became an even bigger disaster than the original attempted intelligence operation.

Since that time, the continued secrecy over the events has led to an ever-increasing number of sometimes bizarre theories as to what actually happened, not only during Cdr Crabb's fatal dive but over the two mysterious appearances of a body eventually recovered in Chichester Harbour, 14 months later.

The following examples are representative of the diversity of these theories.

THEORY 1:   HE WAS SHOT BY A SOVIET MARKSMAN WHEN HE
              SURFACED BETWEEN THE VESSELS

Don Hale in his book *The Final Dive* described how a Russian Naval Intelligence Officer contacted an Israeli journalist named Igal Sarna in Tel Aviv and told him that one of the crew of the *Ordzhonikidze* saw Cdr Crabb surface and shot him and then his body sank.

THEORY 2:   HE WAS MURDERED BY A SOVIET FROGMAN

In November 2007 an ex-Russian frogman named Eduard Koltsov appeared on a Russian TV documentary claiming to have killed Cdr Crabb. He claimed that he caught Cdr Crabb attaching a mine to the side of the cruiser at the location of its ammunition store. He attacked him and cut his throat with his diving knife.

Eduard Koltsov appeared on Russian television claiming to be an ex-frogman and had killed Cdr Crabb with his knife.

21

THEORY 3:   HE WAS CAUGHT BY SOVIET FROGMEN AND ABDUCTED
            TO RUSSIA

One of the most popular theories is that Cdr Crabb somehow ended up alive and well in Russia. Bernard Hutton first promoted the theory that Cdr Crabb had gone to Russia in his books *Frogman Spy* and *The Fake Defector*. This has also been the theory promulgated by Mike Welham in his books. Once in Russia, Cdr Crabb joined the Soviet navy under the name of Commander Lev Lvovich Korablov and served at the Frogman Squadron of the Naval Training Command at Kronstadt.

The explanation of how he got to Russia varies but one theory was that Cdr Crabb had been caught near the Soviet cruiser by Soviet frogmen and dragged into an underwater air-lock. A naval officer and Petty officer claimed to have seen the struggle on the surface. Cdr Crabb was then imprisoned on the ship and taken back to Russia. He was brainwashed and persuaded to work for the Russian navy.

THEORY 4:   HE DELIBERATELY BOARDED THE SOVIET CRUISER
            TO DEFECT

There are two versions of this theory. The first is that Cdr Crabb had become a communist sympathizer and deliberately gave himself up to the Russians on the Soviet cruiser, perhaps entering via an underwater air-lock. He thus defected to Russia and voluntarily offered his services to the Soviets.

This theory was suggested by Sydney Knowles in his book *A Diver in the Dark*. He had been concerned about Crabb's association with known Soviet sympathisers, including Anthony Blunt.

The second version is that Cdr Crabb deliberately allowed himself to be captured, as part of a MI6 plot, and taken to Russia where he worked for the Soviet navy. It was then intended that he escaped back to Britain bringing valuable intelligence on Soviet underwater capabilities with him. But for some reason the escape never took place.

Left: A picture allegedly showing Cdr Crabb (*left*) in the Russian navy.

Below: Sir Anthony Blunt, who was a communist spy and was later stripped of his knighthood.

THEORY 5:   CDR CRABB DIED ABOARD THE RUSSIAN CRUISER

A former naval officer has suggested that Cdr Crabb died of respiratory problems after having been taken onboard the *Ordzhonikidze*. He was subsequently buried at sea with full military honours.

THEORY 6:   THE BODY FOUND IN CHICHESTER HARBOUR HAD BEEN DUMPED FROM A SOVIET SUBMARINE

J Bernard Hutton described in his book *The Fake Defector* how the Russians prepared a body, allowed it to decompose for over a year and then released it from a Soviet submarine off the entrance to Chichester harbour on 6 June 1957, on its way to Egypt. The purpose was to deflect suspicion that Cdr Crabb was still alive and secretly working for the Russians.

THEORY 7: HE WAS KILLED BY AN SBS DIVER

Sydney Knowles proposed this theory in his book *A Diver in the Dark* in 2009. He stated that an SBS diver had been sent to kill Cdr Crabb during the mission to eliminate him as a liability to the government. He further theorised that the assassination went wrong. The two frogmen killed each other and the two bodies which were fished up in Chichester harbour were those of Cdr Crabb and the SBS diver.

THEORY 8: HE WAS KILLED BY THE ISRAELI SECRET SERVICE MOSSAD

Cdr Crabb had worked in Haifa, Israel, between 1945 and 1947. A militant Zionist group Irgun was attacking British warships and merchant ships and Cdr Crabb was detailed to establish another Underwater Working Party similar to the one he had led in Gibraltar during WW2. Mossad agents, in an act of revenge, had tampered with Cdr Crabb's breathing set which resulted in his death.

THEORY 9: SOVIET SPIES TAMPERED WITH CDR CRABB'S BREATHING SET

A similar theory was proposed by Don Hale in his book *The Final Dive* whereby Soviet spies had tampered with Cdr Crabb's breathing set.

THEORY 10: CDR CRABB DIED ON THE STEPS OF KING'S STAIRS

A naval officer has stated that Cdr Crabb returned from his dive to King's Stairs (from where he said he had set off) in an exhausted condition and died in his arms.

THEORY 11: CDR CRABB WAS STRUCK BY A PASSING OIL TANKER

A small oil tanker or "oiler" boat (No 653) came alongside South Railway Jetty unannounced, near where HMS *Maidstone's* launch was berthed at the time that Cdr Crabb made his dive on the morning of 19 April. It had no permission to tie up and was sent away again. It has been suggested that Cdr Crabb may have been hit by the oiler's propeller and killed.

THEORY 12: CDR CRABB WAS ELECTROCUTED BY STEEL NETTING
UNDER THE RUSSIAN SHIPS

THEORY 13: CDR CRABB DIED BECAUSE OF A MALFUNCTION OF HIS
BREATHING APPARATUS

There are several possible modes of failure of any closed circuit[3] oxygen breathing apparatus with consequential serious effects. One such mode of failure was if the Protosorb[4] chemical filling was not correctly packed when the canister was freshly charged, channelling could occur, whereby a proportion of the expired gas would pass directly through the canister without passing through the Protosorb granules and thus fail to have the carbon dioxide removed completely. This could lead to a dangerous carbon dioxide build-up in the breathing circuit.

A classic mode of failure with the single hose arrangement was a "soda-lime cocktail" whereby in the event of water leaking into the mask and running down into the Protosorb canister, a highly caustic foam can be produced which expands up the breathing hose and can enter the mouth and even lungs of the diver. The result is painful and can render the breathing apparatus unusable, with fatal results.

The following sections attempt to provide as near a factual account as possible. The reader may then be in a position to form an opinion of his/her own and to judge how reasonable the author's conclusions may be. In the meantime, the continued secrecy will continue to feed our speculation.

---

[3] A closed circuit breathing apparatus is one where the diver's breathing gas is re-circulated 100% (rather than being vented into the water).

[4] 'Protosorb' is a proprietary name for a commercial form of soda lime. It is used to absorb carbon dioxide exhaled by the diver.

The Cdr Crabb/MI6 diving operation

To avoid tedious repetition, the word 'allegedly' should be assumed to be used in most of the sentences below.

On 22 February 1956 a meeting was held at the Admiralty to discuss the rare opportunity for intelligence procurement presented by Russian naval visits to Western European ports.

In mid-March 1956 another meeting was held at the Admiralty about intelligence operations to be carried out against the Russian warships due to visit Portsmouth, and specifically included the use of frogmen.

Also in March 1956 Cdr Crabb was invited to a meeting at Cowdray Park attended by the First Sea Lord (1954–1959), Admiral of the Fleet, The Earl Mountbatten of Burma.

Sir Edward Bridges confirmed that Cdr Crabb was approached around mid-March to see if he would be willing to carry out the diving operation, presumably by MI6.

Cdr Crabb was subsequently commissioned by MI6/SIS to undertake a dive under the Soviet cruiser for a fee of £100.

MONDAY, 16 APRIL 1956

The late Mike Borrow related a story that on the morning of the 16th, Cdr Crabb called in to see him at his office on the second floor, 91 Regent Street, London where they chatted over a cup of coffee. At that time Borrow was working as the Sales Manager of P Frankenstein & Sons Ltd, a division of Beaufort (Air-Sea) Equipment Ltd, which produced Safety, Escape and Survival gear for submarine and high altitude applications. They then walked round to Chez Marcel's drinking club, opposite the New Theatre in St Martin's Lane. This was a candle-lit, upstairs club that had become popular for some time with bomb and mine disposal personnel when in London. They never discussed Cdr Crabb's diving projects and Mike had assumed that he was then simply selling furniture and fittings to new coffee bars on a commission basis (see Appendix 2: Maitland Pendock)

TUESDAY, 17 APRIL 1956

In the morning, Cdr Crabb said goodbye to Miss Amy Thomas, the manageress of the flats at 2 Hans Road saying he would be back in a few days. He then went round to his fiancée's apartment, Pat Rose who has been described as a "society beauty". At about 13.00 hours they went to the Nag's Head public house in Kinnerton Street for lunch. This was one of Cdr Crabb's favourite pubs and he knew the landlord, Len Cole, well. According to Cole they called in the pub on an almost daily basis. On this occasion Cdr Crabb drank only half a pint of beer and only picked at his food.

Above: Pat Rose, Cdr Crabb's fiancée at the time of his disappearance.

Right: The Nag's Head in Kinnerton Street, Knightsbridge, which Cdr Crabb and Pat Rose frequently visited.

Accompanied by Matthew Smith of MI6 (aka Ted Davies, aka Bernard Sydney Smith) he took a train to Portsmouth arriving in the evening. Smith has been described as a tall, well dressed man, thirty one years old with dark hair and a moustache. He had a Master of Arts degree from Trinity College, Oxford. He was fluent in both German and Russian and spoke with an American accent. This has led to speculation that he was actually a CIA agent. Another source claimed that Ted Davies was a former RNVR officer who headed the MI6 naval liaison unit, Section R3 in Vauxhall Bridge Road, London, responsible to Nicholas Elliott.

According to Len Cole and Pat Rose, she also accompanied Cdr Crabb to Portsmouth on the train and then caught the next train back to London. This conflicts with Pat Rose's comment that she was with Cdr Crabb the night before he disappeared. She had met Smith about two weeks earlier and took an immediate dislike to him, adding he spoke "like an American". Cdr Crabb and Smith proceeded to the Sally Port Hotel where they registered with their own names and addresses. Smith gave his address as "Attached Foreign Office".

The same evening Cdr Crabb and Smith held a meeting with Chief Constable Arthur Charles West OBE at his offices in a mock Tudor mansion on the corner of Kent Road and Queens Crescent, Southsea. They then moved to the then City Central Police Station in the vicarage in St Michael's Road, Southsea. They were given a scrambler telephone and assigned Chief Detective Superintendent Jack Lamport as their liaison officer.

Later, Cdr Crabb made several telephone calls. He telephoned his employer Maitland Pendock; and later that evening he telephoned Lt Cdr George Albert 'Frankie' Franklin, senior Clearance Diver at the Diving School in HMS *Vernon*. They arranged to meet for a drink at a pub near to where Franklin lived. Once there, Cdr Crabb asked Franklin to assist him with his dive the following day. Franklin has stated he was asked whether:

Left: The Sally Port Hotel, in the High Street, Portsmouth where Cdr Crabb stayed prior to his disappearance.

Below: The principal locations in Portsmouth and Gosport.

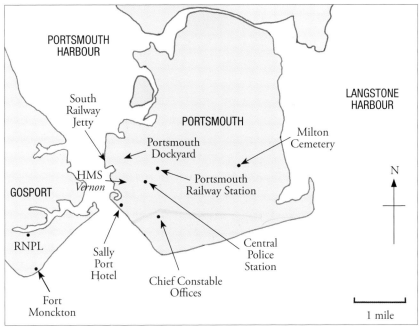

PORTSMOUTH HARBOUR

LANGSTONE HARBOUR

South Railway Jetty

PORTSMOUTH

Milton Cemetery

Portsmouth Dockyard

N

HMS *Vernon*

Portsmouth Railway Station

GOSPORT

RNPL

Sally Port Hotel

Central Police Station

Fort Monckton

Chief Constable Offices

1 mile

Right: The 'vicarage' in St Michael's Road, Southsea, where the Central Police Station was housed and where Cdr Crabb met Superintendent Jack Lamport.

Below: The mock Tudor mansion in Queen's Crescent, Portsmouth where Cdr Crabb went to meet Chief Constable West.

"… I would be prepared to assist him entirely unofficially and in a strictly private capacity in connection with a dive he was undertaking a day or two later, the nature of which was not disclosed to me, and I was told by commander Crabb that on no account was I to inform any responsible Naval Authority; I agreed on my own responsibility."

Franklin's statement was heavily influenced by W A Lewen, Assistant Head of Naval Law at the Admiralty and was clearly taken with the view to emphasising his involvement as being entirely unofficial and outside his naval duties. The Admiralty needed to show they were not involved in the Cdr Crabb/Naval Intelligence operation. However, they were not entirely uninvolved. A note to the Prime Minister dated 8 June 1956 stated:

"It is clear that the frogman operation was never regarded in the Admiralty as a naval responsibility and the Admiralty's concern with it was limited from the outset to providing "unofficial facilities" such as access to the dockyard."

The "unofficial facilities" presumably also included the use of HMS *Maidstone*'s launch (from which Crabb dived) and the loan of an oxygen rebreather set. However it is not known at what level this assistance was authorised. It may have been at Cdr Crabb's level where he was simply calling in favours from old friends such as Lt Cdr Franklin.

During the debate in Parliament on 14 May 1956 on 'The Case of Commander Crabb', Mr John Dugdale MP stated:

"Commander Crabb asked to borrow equipment from HMS Vernon and he was refused. It was said there. 'We shall not lend you the equipment'. Obviously, he wanted accommodation of the most convenient character, and, naturally, he would have stayed in an Admiralty establishment … but the Admiralty did not want him to do so and the Commander-in-Chief, Portsmouth, did not want him to. So he had to resort to this extraordinary business of staying in an hotel, and signing the register, while his companion signed it with the wrong name."

This indicates that knowledge of Cdr Crabb's planned diving operation existed in the Admiralty at least up to the level of the C-in-C, Portsmouth, Admiral of the Fleet, Sir George Creasy.

Cdr Crabb had previously asked Gutteridge's Second-in-Command, Lt Mark Terrell to assist him with his dive but Terrell had turned him down. Cdr Crabb had also asked Sydney Knowles to help him but he had also turned him down. Knowles could not see any reason to undertake the dive, having surveyed the cruiser's sister ship, the *Sverdlov* with Cdr Crabb in October the previous year.

Surprisingly, it appears that Cdr Crabb still had not arranged to have any assistance for his dive by the time he approached Franklin, the day before his planned dive. This was a little late in the day to be making such important arrangements. It confirms that the planning of the operation left something to be desired. It also indicates that MI6 were relying on Cdr Crabb to make his own arrangements for assistance with the diving operation.

Cdr Crabb returned to the Sally Port Hotel where he and Smith stayed overnight.

WEDNESDAY, 18 APRIL 1956

On schedule, at around 10.45 hours in the morning, the Soviet cruiser *Ordzhonikidze* accompanied by two destroyers, the *Sovershenny* and the *Smotryashchie* arrived at the Outer Spit Buoy, just outside Portsmouth Harbour. They proceeded into the harbour, passing through the narrow entrance shortly before 11.00 hours. The tide was flooding gently, following low water at 09.49 hours. The *Ordzhonikidze* was the first to tie up at the South Railway Jetty, starboard side on, with her bow pointing to the north. It was followed at ten-minute intervals, first by the *Sovershenny* and then the *Smotryashchie* which tied up alongside the cruiser. Just ahead of the Soviet vessels, the aircraft carrier, HMS *Bulwark* was berthed, at Pitch House Jetty. At 11.50 hours a 19 gun salute was fired from HMS *Bulwark* in honour of Marshall Bulganin.

The *Ordzhonikidze* was 210 metres long and (importantly) had a draft of 6.9 metres (23 feet). It occupied the entire length of the South Railway Jetty.

Cdr Crabb had originally intended to carry out some preparations for his dive in the dockyard that morning (or perhaps even a dive according to Bridges) but had been prevented from getting in by the intense security precautions at the time. These were in place to cover the transfer arrangements for Bulganin and Khrushchev that morning, from the cruiser to the railway station, on their way to London to meet the Prime Minister. Nobody was allowed on the South Railway Jetty except the official party and members of the press who had been able to secure passes. A Royal Navy helicopter circled above the Soviet warships. Police numbers in the dockyard were considerably strengthened. Outside the dockyard, police lined the short route to the station. Portsmouth's Chief Constable A C West was responsible for the visitors' security outside the dockyard.

Mary Barnett, the Clerical Officer at AEDU.

Instead, Cdr Crabb visited HMS *Vernon* in the morning. He went to the Admiralty Experimental Diving Unit (AEDU, Appendix 3) where amongst others he met the Clerical Officer, Mary Barnett, with whom he was on very good terms. It has been suggested that Barnett, who had joined the AEDU staff in 1954 had assisted in providing Cdr Crabb with his oxygen breathing set.

He went to the Officers' Wardroom at *Vernon* where he met John Emm, a wardroom steward, and asked to borrow his car to transport an oxygen breathing apparatus from *Vernon's* dive store. In the afternoon, Cdr Crabb had tea with Cdr Emmerson, former executive officer of *Vernon*.

High water at Portsmouth Harbour was 17.35 hours (Hydrographic Office Tables). It was a neap tide.

Lt Cdr Franklin drove Cdr Crabb to the Dockyard and to the waterside where a launch from HMS *Maidstone* (Appendix 5) was tied up in the Boat Pound (also known as the "South Camber"), immediately south of South Railway Jetty.

At 17.30 hours Cdr Crabb entered the water from the launch. The stern of the Soviet cruiser was conveniently just around the corner of the South Railway Jetty. It is not known who had arranged the use of the launch, but it was presumably fairly well in advance of the ill-fated project.

Franklin assisted Cdr Crabb to dress in his Heinke two-piece dry suit, fins and oxygen equipment in the launch, following which, Cdr Crabb slipped over the side and disappeared underwater. He had to swim along the side of the jetty, across the pilings and then turn to the right at the corner. This would have been effectively in total darkness and zero visibility.

At 18.00 hours approximately, Cdr Crabb returned to the launch and Franklin assisted him back onboard. The attempt had been abortive. According to Cdr Emmerson, Cdr Crabb had become "*entangled in the pilings of the jetty*". Cdr Crabb decided to try another dive early the next day at the next high water slack, with some additional weight. Lt Cdr Franklin had noted that Cdr Crabb had used very little oxygen and that he "*... appeared to be in good trim.*"

Cdr Crabb should have known his weighting requirements. Being incorrectly weighted was a sign of inadequate preparation.

In the author's view, apart from the challenge of navigating between them in zero visibility, the pilings themselves would not have presented a problem. However there may well have been debris amongst the pilings.

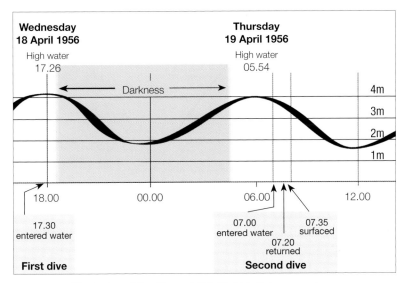

The timing of the tides and Cdr Crabb's diving operations.

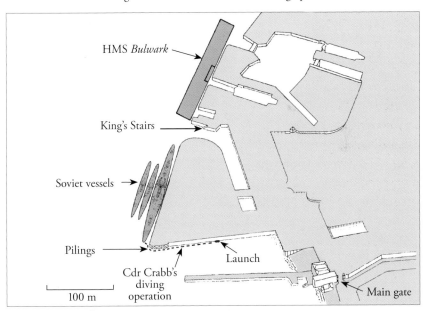

Map showing the location of Cdr Crabb's diving operation.

HMS *Maidstone* berthed at South Railway Jetty shortly after the Russian vessels had departed. Note the locations of HMS *Bulwark* and the launch.

The pilings at South Railway Jetty around which Cdr Crabb had to navigate in zero visibility during his diving operations.

An Admiralty note following the incident addressing the problem of searching for Cdr Crabb's body, declared that:

"an inspection of the space under the jetty [by divers] *would be a dangerous operation because of obstructions, wire ropes, old anchors etc."*

These would have certainly been a problem for a diver operating in poor visibility conditions.

Assuming Cdr Crabb used the same oxygen set the following day, someone had to refill the oxygen cylinders using a hand-pump and re-charge the Protosorb canister that evening. That could have been done onboard HMS *Maidstone* berthed further up the harbour at North Corner Jetty or back at HMS *Vernon*.

At around 18.00 hours, local resident John Towse happened to be crossing the harbour on the Gosport ferry on his way to night school in Portsmouth. It was dusk and he saw activity on the stern of the cruiser where a group of sailors were assembled shining powerful torches and pointing down towards the water. The local newspaper reported:

"Miniature searchlights blazed out over Portsmouth Harbour Wednesday from the sterns of the Soviet vessels ... they lit up the waters immediately to the rear of the three warships ..."

"... search-lights blazed from the sterns of the three ships as they lay at the South Railway Jetty ... The lights did not range about but were concentrated at the rear of the three vessels."

In light of the circumstances, this strongly suggests that the Russians had detected suspicious activity near the stern of the cruiser. It is quite possible that Cdr Crabb's under-weighting problem had caused him to momentarily rise too close to the surface. However, no positive sighting was reported.

In the evening, Cdr Crabb went to The Bear Hotel in Havant and met Lt Cdr John Crawford and his wife Daphne together with PO 'Lofty' Gordon (who was in charge of the Vernon Diving Store). Crawford had been the first to be trained up as a Clearance Diver

The Bear Hotel,
High Street,
Havant.

(CD) in HMS *Lochinvar*, Scotland, by Lt Gordon Gutteridge and
Cdr Bob Harland before he moved to *Vernon* and established the CD
school there.

THURSDAY, 19 APRIL 1956

High water at Portsmouth was at 06.01 hours and it was a neap tide
(a small range of rise and fall).

Just before 06.00 hours Cdr Crabb and Smith left the Sally Port
Hotel and met up with Lt Cdr Franklin. They entered the dockyard
escorted by Supt Lamport. Smith and Franklin boarded the launch
from HMS *Maidstone* still moored at the Boat Pound about 70 metres
(80 yards) from the cruiser. The two police officers then left.

Shortly before 07.00 hours Cdr Crabb, assisted by Franklin, left
the surface having put on additional lead weights. His oxygen supply
and carbon dioxide absorbent were estimated to be capable of lasting
about one and a half hours, or two hours maximum. He was expected
to return in less than one hour.

Cdr Crabb was an unfit, 47-year-old, heavy smoking near alcoholic. He was using pure oxygen which he knew to be toxic when breathed at depth. The fit young divers of the Royal Navy were restricted to a depth of 7 metres (23 feet) for this reason. Physical effort, such as active swimming and lack of fitness reduces a diver's tolerance. Cdr Crabb was therefore diving to the limits of oxygen tolerance even for fit young men.

Furthermore, there was a possible danger of carbon dioxide poisoning because he was wearing a Pattern 5562 SWBA (see p.62) with a single hose which operated on a 'pendulum breathing' principle. This term refers to the rebreathing of the gas contained in the 'dead space' of the hose from the carbon dioxide canister with each breathing cycle. It necessitates the diver having to avoid breathing shallow breaths. This becomes a serious problem if the diver starts to pant, ie, becomes out of breath.

Both conditions, oxygen or carbon dioxide poisoning, lead to unconsciousness followed usually by drowning or asphyxia.

Despite all these challenging and danger factors, Cdr Crabb characteristically committed himself to the underwater investigation without reservation or concern for his own life.

According to Lt Cdr Franklin, he was wearing:
– cotton vest
– bathing trunks, maroon
– rayon combinations, service issue, fawn/khaki
– stockinet combinations
– socks
– little woolly balaclava with bathing cap on top
– Heinke two piece diving suit
– Rubber flippers
– Breathing apparatus, 90 minutes comfortable endurance, two hours maximum.

The Heinke two-piece dry suit, the type that Cdr Crabb preferred. The illustration shows a 'hood-attached' version whereas Cdr Crabb used a version with a neck seal.

At about 07.20 hours, Cdr Crabb returned to the launch having failed to achieve his objective. He was out of breath and cold. He complained that the visibility was bad. Franklin checked the equipment and Cdr Crabb re-entered the water. It has to be assumed that Cdr Crabb had experienced serious difficulties during his short dive, otherwise he would not have returned to the launch.

When he recommenced the dive he was therefore, in addition to having already used up part of his oxygen supply and carbon dioxide absorbent, he was now also in a cold and tired condition inevitably accompanied by a significant level of stress. Being unfit, relatively old, out of breath and cold means that his resistance to oxygen and carbon dioxide poisoning would have been reduced.

He had missed high water slack and the tide was beginning to ebb. He would have been obliged to swim against a slight current as soon as he reached the corner of the jetty and ventured under the hull of the cruiser. The current would have been accelerated where the tidal stream was forced through the gap between the hull and the sea bed.

He dived around high water, so the sea surface was about 4 metres above chart datum. The area was dredged to 10 metres (33 feet) below chart datum, giving a total water depth of 14 metres (46 feet). The cruiser's draught was 6.9 metres which, by coincidence happened to be the maximum safe diving depth using oxygen apparatus whilst swimming.

At around 07.30 to 08.00 hours, three Soviet sailors on the *Sovershenny* observed a diver, face-up on the surface for one or two minutes, between the sterns of the two destroyers. One report suggested he appeared to be in difficulties. The diver then resubmerged under the *Smotryashchie*, the outermost of the two destroyers. It may be safely assumed that this would have been Cdr Crabb. To have surfaced means that he was certainly in serious trouble. Furthermore, since his objective was specifically to investigate the propellers and rudder of the cruiser *Ordzhonikidze*, surfacing between the two destroyers (which was beyond his planned range of operation) suggests that Cdr Crabb had also become disorientated and lost his bearings.

Sir Edward Bridges reported that on 21 April:

"Admiral Kotov who had spent the day informally with Admiral Burnett (Chief of Staff to the Chief-in-Command (C-in-C), Portsmouth) said, over the coffee after dinner, that three of his sailors had seen a frogman about 8 o'clock in the morning of the 19th, but he was not proposing to make a fuss about it or to lodge a complaint."

Nicholas Elliott has stated:

"The Soviet admiral was entertaining the Commander-in-Chief Portsmouth to drinks on board his ship and said to him that his officer of the watch had reported that a diver had been seen in trouble round the stern of the ship that morning and he hoped he was alright. The admiral did not appear to take this in any way amiss (he lodged no formal or informal protest) ..."

The Soviet politicians took a different view and the Soviet Embassy complained to the Foreign Office in a note dated 5 May 1956, though not in particularly strong terms. Indeed it was more of an observation than a complaint:

"... at 7.30 hours on April 19, three sailors of the Soviet vessels discovered a diver swimming between the Soviet destroyers at their moorings at the South River Jetty. The diver, dressed in a black light-diving suit with floats [sic] *on his feet, was on the surface of the water for the space of one or two minutes and then dived again, under the destroyer Smotryashchie."*

For the diver to have surfaced and remained there for such a long time under such circumstances indicates that the he was in serious difficulties. These were almost certainly life-threatening difficulties. In my opinion, this was very likely to have been Cdr Crabb in very serious trouble.

Nobody ever saw Cdr Crabb alive again.

At 09.15 hours Franklin searched for Cdr Crabb in *Maidstone's* launch without success. He has stated that:

"... during their search, they neither heard or saw any sign of abnormal activities from the Russians."

The use of the launch for a search suggests that it was crewed by one or more men from HMS *Maidstone*, very likely from their diving instructor team.

Smith eventually went to inform the Chief Constable and the Naval Intelligence Division representative at Portsmouth of the problem. The latter arranged a further search with a motor launch but without success. Lt Cdr Franklin informed the Captain of HMS *Vernon*, Captain E A Blundell, who immediately acquainted the Commander-in-Chief, Portsmouth, Admiral of the Fleet, Sir George E Creasy. At 11.30 hours Smith collected Cdr Crabb's gear from the Sally Port Hotel, paid the bill and returned to London.

Hugh Winterborne and John Henry of MI5 and MI6 respectively went to Portsmouth to tie up loose ends.

SATURDAY, 21 APRIL

Detective-Superintendent Jack Lamport, head of Portsmouth CID removed two pages from the register of the Sally Port Hotel, High Street, Portsmouth.

TUESDAY, 24 APRIL

Maitland Pendock, Cdr Crabb's employer in London, rang Lt Cdr John Crawford in Havant to ask about Cdr Crabb's whereabouts. Crawford then made enquiries at the Admiralty.

WEDNESDAY, 25 APRIL

The decision was taken at the Admiralty that "the top priority was to prevent the story breaking while the Russians were still in England," just two more days.

Vice Chief of Naval Staff, Vice-Admiral Sir William Davis KCB DSO approved that Captain Sarell RN should be sent to meet Maitland Pendock to try to persuade him to keep quiet.

FRIDAY, 27 APRIL

Superintendent Lamport of the Portsmouth Police visited the Sally Port Hotel and, acting on the orders of the Chief Constable, A C West (ie, not at the request of MI6 – according to MI6), removed two pages from the hotel register, bearing the details of Cdr Crabb and Smith.

Captain Sarell RN was sent by the Admiralty to inform Cdr Crabb's mother, Mrs Beatrice 'Daisy' Crabb, of his presumed death.

This was also the last day of the Soviet visit and the three warships left Portsmouth Harbour.

SATURDAY, 28 APRIL

Captain Sarell was sent to discuss matters with Mrs Margaret Crabb, Cdr Crabb's ex-wife. MI6 wanted to keep the incident under wraps and especially away from the press.

SUNDAY, 29 APRIL

Having been tipped off by either Cdr Crabb's friends or relatives, the press first began to ask questions of the Admiralty.

The Admiralty announced that Cdr Crabb was presumed dead after failing to return from an underwater trial at Stokes Bay.

MONDAY, 30 APRIL

Speculative reports about Cdr Crabb's disappearance appeared in the press. The Times reported:

"The Admiralty stated last night: 'He did not return from a test dive which took place in connexion with trials of certain underwater apparatus in Stokes Bay, in the Portsmouth area, about a week ago."

WEDNESDAY, 2 MAY

Daily Mail reporters discovered that the pages had been removed from the Sally Port Hotel register.

THURSDAY, 3 MAY

The morning papers gave considerable publicity to the hotel register incident and an all-out, national press campaign was launched.

FRIDAY, 4 MAY

A furious Prime Minister was belatedly informed of what had happened after first reading about it in the press.

Marshall Pugh who had been working with Cdr Crabb on writing his biography told the press that he had received an assurance that Cdr Crabb "had died on service".

The Visitor Registration Book at the Sally Port Hotel where Cdr Crabb stayed during his diving operations in Portsmouth.

The Russians hand-delivered a note of protest to the Foreign Office in the evening.

THURSDAY, 10 MAY

The *Evening News* of Portsmouth reported:

"... *there has been dredging on both sides of King's Stairs. This is probably routine work, although no-one will deny that it could be for the purpose of searching for a body or for equipment.*"

FRIDAY, 11 MAY

The Russian newspapers *Pravda* and *Izvestiya* carry articles about Cdr Crabb.

MONDAY, 14 MAY

The Chief Constable of the crime office in Chichester wrote to all local police authorities in Portsmouth area warning them that should Cdr Crabb's body surface:

"It is absolutely essential that the finding of the body is not to be disclosed to the press."

Labour MP Mr Zilliacus speculated in *The Times*:

The most likely explanation is the possibility that Commander Crabb, who had retired but was still taken on from time to time for special jobs, had on this occasion been employed by the United States secret service with the complicity of their – and his – contacts in the British secret service.

An Admiralty note stated:

Crabb is believed to have been in debt to the tune of many hundreds of pounds, probably £2,200–£3,000; These include arrears in alimony (about £500), divorce case costs (£120). There are no known assets, except for a share of royalties from his biography by a friend Pugh … We believe he died intestate … There is a statutory provision for the Admiralty to notify the Registrar General of deaths of naval officers and men … if this procedure is to be followed, a certain amount of "wangling" will be involved … If the body turns up … there will be an inquest – in the place where the body is found.

A little later, in July it was reported that Cdr Crabb left £1,205 gross, £374 net.

FRIDAY, 25 MAY

G F Marshall, Chief Engineer in Charge at the dockyard gave his opinion on the practicalities of a search for Cdr Crabb's body under South Railway Jetty. Dredging would take 10 days at a cost of about £3,500. A diver search would be:

"… very laborious owing to debris. A quick look along the front of the jetty could be done in 5 days probably at a cost of about £60, A proper inspection of the whole space under the jetty would take 3 to 4 weeks or perhaps even more at about £50/60 a week."

He added:

"The underside of the jetty is encumbered with wire ropes and other debris. The tidal stream on ebb and flow sets in towards the jetty and there are local eddies which maintain a northward flow after high water … If anything is there I would personally think its most probable location is caught up in debris near the front of the jetty.

Did Cdr Crabb dive on his own?

In reply to the question put to the Admiralty, *"What precautions are normally taken in a trial of this nature and were they taken on this occasion?"*

The Admiralty replied, *"Normally two divers would be used and a safety boat would be in attendance."*

This is consistent with the arrangements made for the Royal Naval dive where at least two divers carried out the investigation, operating from a diving tender. However, whilst it appears that Cdr Crabb operated from a launch from HMS *Maidstone*, there has not been any evidence disclosed that would indicate he had a buddy diver.

If Cdr Crabb had been diving with a buddy diver, he would have been on a 'buddy line' in order to have been able to remain in contact with him in bad visibility water. In such a case, when Cdr Crabb got in to trouble, he could (and surely would) have been recovered by the buddy diver.

The author's conclusion is therefore that on the balance of probabilities Cdr Crabb dived alone.

How did Cdr Crabb die?

Cdr Crabb was a prime contender for death by oxygen or carbon dioxide poisoning followed by asphyxia or drowning. In my view this is the most likely explanation. He could even have died of natural causes, such as a heart attack.

Alternatively Cdr Crabb could have been stunned by the operation of the powerful sonar equipment on any one or all three of the vessels, followed by drowning or asphyxia. Indeed, there were several anti-diver options open to the Russians.

However, it is most unlikely that the Russians would have wanted to take any such drastic action, not least because it could have endangered the lives of RN divers carrying out 'legitimate' work in the vicinity. According to the late Mike Borrow OBE, who had met several Soviet naval officers in the ensuing years, including an assistant naval attaché who had been serving on the *Ordzhonikidze* at the time of Cdr Crabb's dive, they had always taken it for granted that Royal Navy divers inspected all their ships whilst visiting UK ports. Peter Wright (*Spycatcher*) stated that the KGB even had advance notice of Cdr Crabb's intended dive. Chapman Pincher (*Treachery*) has stated that " ... *Soviet Intelligence had a month's advance warning of Cdr Crabb's operation.*"

The Soviets themselves had equivalent objectives. When British warships had visited Leningrad the previous year, in October, 1955, "*they were subjected to intensive intelligence probes by the Russians, including the use of divers.*"

In the event, the Soviets made no more than a nominal fuss about the observed diver activities near their vessels. They certainly did not exploit the matter for any political gains or allow it to interfere with the main diplomatic objective of their visit.

Were the CIA involved in Cdr Crabb's diving operation?

The original idea that the Central Intelligence Agency (CIA) of the USA were involved in the Cdr Crabb/MI6 operation arose out of Pat Rose's observation that Mr Smith, who accompanied Cdr Crabb from London to Portsmouth and stayed at the Sally Port Hotel with him, spoke with an American accent.

The author's enquiry to the CIA requesting information about any involvement in the Cdr Crabb affair under the US Freedom of Information Act drew the following unhelpful response: *"In accordance with section 3.6(a) of Executive Order 13526, the CIA can neither confirm nor deny the existence or non existence of records responsive to your request."*

A letter from the Admiralty to Sir John Lang hurriedly sent immediately following the Inquest, quoted the Crabb family solicitor who stated: *"... every particle of evidence in our possession points conclusively to the fact that this very gallant gentleman died as he had lived in the service of our country and of no other."*

The Admiralty commented: *"Statement seems to have been aimed at earlier puff that Crabb was working for American agency."*

Looking at the diving operation objectively, there does not seem to have been any advantage in including a CIA operative directly. It would have been an entirely unnecessary complication to an already ill-prepared mission. This is especially so since the whole operation depended heavily on Cdr Crabb's personal contacts and local influence. Cdr Crabb's associate would have had to have been a bona fide MI6 agent.

In view of the lack of any convincing evidence, in the author's opinion on the balance of probabilities the CIA were not involved in Cdr Crabb's diving operation.

The Royal Navy / Naval Intelligence diving operation

The most recent releases of classified information on the Cdr Crabb affair under the Freedom of Information Act in October 2006, have revealed that the Naval Intelligence Division commissioned a duplicate investigation of the Soviet cruiser using at least two pairs of naval divers about the same time. Naval Intelligence were especially interested in the underwater noise characteristics of the *Ordzhonikidze* and whether there were any special provisions for reducing the cavitation noise of the propellers.

The late Lt Cdr Joe Brooks[5] DSC was at the time in command of the Clearance Diving Acceptance Trials Team at *Vernon* (as opposed to the Development Trials Team attached to the Underwater Countermeasures & Weapons Establishment (UCWE) in Havant, where Cdr Crabb had worked). The latter developed equipment that the former then tested before being introduced into service. Several sources claim that Joe Brooks was in charge of, and the lead diver who investigated the cruiser. Brooks himself enthusiastically did not deny being involved to his friends. He and his team were based onboard HMS *Deepwater* (Appendix 4) permanently berthed at HMS

Lt Cdr Joe Brooks DSC who was in charge of the clearance diving acceptance trials team.

---

[5] Joe Brooks had distinguished himself during WW2 when he carried out a successful attack in Bergen with X-craft X.24, for which he had been awarded the DSC.

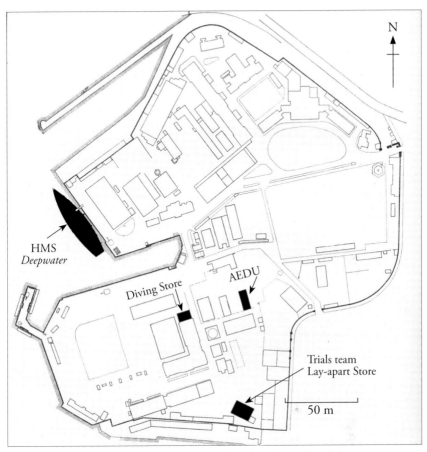

HMS *Vernon*, Portsmouth, which included AEDU and the
diving school onboard HMS *Deepwater*.

Vernon shore establishment. Cdr Crabb and Brooks were old friends.
One of Brooks' sons has said he remembers his father and Cdr Crabb
chatting one evening at their home, shortly before the fatal dive. He
didn't recall the content of the discussion, so we may never know if
they ever revealed their planned operations to each other.

Cdr Crabb was actually eligible to work for Naval Intelligence.
They had "two kinds of delicate intelligence operations," those that

directly involved service personnel and gear and those that employed non-service personnel and equipment. Cdr Crabb's name was on the list of divers "not in the service".

It has been reported that the RN operation commenced at about 10.00 hours, on the morning of 18 April, immediately after the three vessels had tied up. Low water was at 09.49 hours. The divers entered the water at the stern of the aircraft carrier HMS *Bulwark* which was berthed 60 metres further up, north of King's Stairs. *Bulwark* had been alongside at Pitch House Jetty since 1 April.

They dived from a diving tender tied up at the stern of the carrier and to all intents and purposes appeared to be undertaking routine maintenance work on the carrier's propellers. The diving tender, flying the NATO flag four diving flag, was in full view of the Soviet cruiser.

Once underwater, the pairs of divers, who were connected together by a 3m (10-foot) buddy line, turned in the opposite direction and swam south just beneath the surface until they reached the Soviet cruiser's hull. From there Brooks and his partner swam the length of the hull as far as the two propellers and back. They met no other divers during their dive and they both returned safely to the diving tender alongside HMS *Bulwark* without any incident. It was said that they came across swim lines strung across the cruiser's hull, connected at each end to the bilge keels on either side of the hull. These would have been useful for the Russian divers to carry out methodical searches of the hull.

More than one pair of RN divers were involved in the investigation of the Soviet vessels. In a letter sent to the Private Secretary at 10 Downing Street, presumed to be from Lt Cdr Brooks, on 27 March 1981, he mentioned: *"I was in charge of the Naval operational team who successfully surveyed the undersides of the Russian ships at the time to ensure that all was either 'safe' or 'unsafe' … There were others* [note plural] *apart from myself, who did the underwater work …"*

He refers to the "Russian ships" [note plural] so it appears that one or both of the destroyers' hulls were also investigated. This indicates at

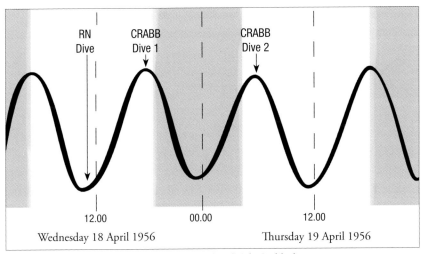

Tidal cycles during the Royal Naval and Cdr Crabb diving operations.

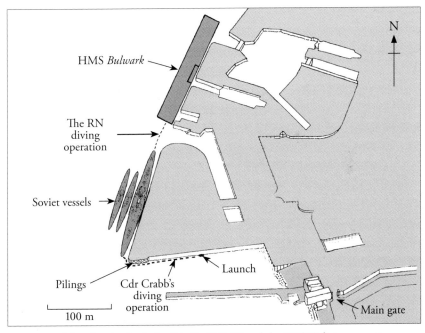

Map showing both the Cdr Crabb/MI6 and the RN/NI diving operations

least one other pair of divers was employed. Indeed the name of Petty Officer Macrae-Clifton has been suggested as one of the other divers.

As in the previous *Sverdlov* investigation, the SIS/MI6 group and the Naval Intelligence group were apparently unaware of the other's involvement.

The reference to "safe or unsafe" is curious. One interpretation of this is that the dive was intended to establish whether there was any nuclear radiation coming from the cruiser.

On 23 April, three days after Cdr Crabb's disappearance, Russian divers were sent down at the stern of the cruiser. They operated from one of the ship's own boats which tied up between the cruiser and the jetty. A newspaper reported: *"They were operating from a ship's boat, and no-one knew what was their purpose. The boat was between the jetty and the cruiser, and the proceedings were watched by a small cluster of Russians on the quarter-deck, and by others on the jetty near the sentry at the gangway. Passing Dockyard men looked on, but nobody had his curiosity satisfied."*

One could speculate that this was in response to suspicions raised on board by the RN dive. The previous day (22 April), the *Ordzhonikidze* had been opened to the public and crowds 30 to 40 deep milled around the single gangway leading on to the cruiser. For the Dockyard police it was a nightmare afternoon. The cruiser was quickly packed with sightseers. On the quayside, three policemen and an English-speaking Russian tried to control the crowds. The Russian sailors would certainly have been kept busy trying to keep control of the crowds on board. Perhaps the opportunity was taken at this particular time to send in the naval diving team and perhaps also this is the reason for the Russian divers to check the stern the following day.

Perhaps more likely, it was in response to having observed Cdr Crabb surfacing three days earlier.

The purpose of the Russian dive could well have been to check that no monitoring devices had been attached to the ship's hull by British divers.

The Bodies

On 14 May 1956 the Chief Constable of the crime office in Chichester wrote to all local police authorities in Portsmouth area warning them that should Cdr Crabb's body surface:

"It is absolutely essential that the finding of the body is not to be disclosed to the press."

It is interesting to note:

a) It was the Chichester Police Station that took this initiative and not Portsmouth.
b) Chichester Police Station belonged to a different force (Sussex) and therefore had no prior involvement in the incident.
c) The body was eventually found in Chichester Harbour.
d) The Chief Constable and Coroner at Chichester were noted by MI6 to be "very co-operative".

BODY NO 1

According to Cole, at around 06.30 hours in the morning of Saturday, 3 November 1956, nearly seven months after Cdr Crabb's disappearance, Emsworth fisherman Harry Cole trawled up a body in his nets whilst fishing. He was on his own and had difficulty recovering the body into the boat. The head fell off in the process and was lost. He could see that it was the body of a diver in a rubber dry suit and it was still wearing a breathing apparatus.

He eventually lost the body again and retained only part of the breathing apparatus which he eventually threw away. Cole did not report this to the police until three months later, on 7 February 1957.

In a statement to the police dated 13 June 1957 he described the equipment he recovered.

"I tried to get the object aboard but owing to the weight it broke away and I was left with a piece of rubber tube, a long rubber strap and a collar. Attached to the collar was a lead weight about four inches by four inches by half an inch."

Cole also drew a sketch to illustrate what he thought the equipment looked like. The sketch is not particularly accurate and it does not conclusively identify exactly what type of apparatus it was. However the sketch shows a single hose connected centrally to the rubber "collar" (assumed to be the breathing bag/counterlung) and a single valve to one side and a weight in a pouch.

Unfortunately, further statements Cole made many years later conflicted with his original version given above. He described two breathing hoses and ball-shaped weights and the discovery was made in the evening. It is likely that the original version given just a few months after the discovery is the closest to the truth.

On Sunday 5 March 1967 a human skull was discovered by walkers partially buried in the sand at Pilsea Sands. The lower jaw was missing but the upper jaw retained seven teeth. The indications of its age and nature of the remaining teeth were consistent with the skull being that of Cdr Crabb. However, the evidence was not conclusive.

Cole has been quoted as saying that after he lost the

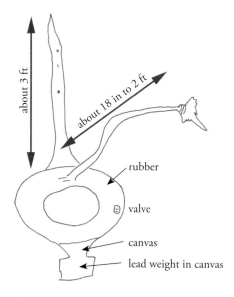

Drawing based on a sketch by Mr Harry Cole showing the remains of the breathing equipment he recovered from the body he picked up in his trawl net.

body it would undoubtedly be fished up again, because anything heavy on the sea bed in that particular part of the harbour tended to remain in that area. If that were the case, then it would add to the attraction of the location to the intelligence agencies for ensuring the eventual discovery and recovery of the body.

BODY NO 2

On Sunday, 9 June 1957, 14 months after Cdr Crabb's disappearance and seven months after the first body had been trawled up from the sea bed, a body was discovered, this time *floating* in Chichester Harbour, 230 m (250 yds) off Pilsea Island. It was found by the crew of a small trawler named *Red Goose*, six tons, from Bosham. There were three fishermen aboard, John Seymour Randall and two brothers, Ted and Bill Gilby. Randall, who lived at Snow Goose, Cutmill, Bosham, had a retail fur business in Portsmouth, by coincidence, near the Sally Port Hotel. They noted the rubber suit was dirty grey, there were rust marks around legs and deep indentations clear of undergrowth where a breathing set may have been attached. They tied it alongside their dingy with an anchor rope and rowed it ashore. At the beach they

John Seymour Randall (in white jumper) and Ted Gilby who discovered Cdr Crabb's body floating in Chichester Harbour.

placed the anchor ashore with the body still floating in the shallows. They proceeded up to the RAF base on Thorney Island and reported their discovery. They were told to return to where the body had been landed and to await the arrival of the police.

The RAF telephoned the police at Southbourne and at 12.00 hours PC Ronald G Williams went to the RAF base on Thorney Island. He and the RAF Medical Officer were transported to the body by members of the 1107 MCU detachment in an old WW2 40ft assault landing craft which was used for inshore and harbour rescue. They included Jim Knight, LAC Ray Howes and one other.

When they arrived they found the body on the beach. They recovered it onto the craft's lowered front ramp and pulled it aboard. It was clear at the time that the head and hands were missing and in the cavity where the head had been were "hundreds of small crabs and

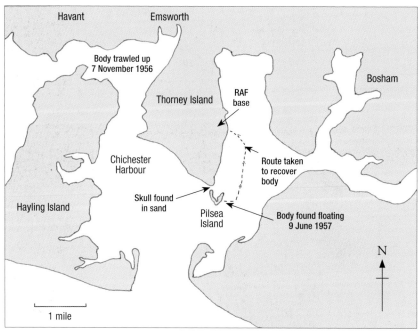

Chichester Harbour showing the locations the bodies were found.

other such creatures. The odour was abominable." They returned to the Marine Craft Section (MCS) and were able to run almost up to West Thorney Road as it was high tide. Waiting for them was a group of RAF Officers including Group Captain Boxer, Station Commander of RAF Thorney, four men in "long dark overcoats" (presumed to be from SIS/MI6), an RAF ambulance, local police and many unknown onlookers. The body was initially taken to the mortuary at Chichester Hospital and then on Tuesday, 11 June, it was transferred to Bognor Mortuary which was more modern and had better refrigeration facilities. The diving suit along with the other items of clothing were retained at Chichester Police Station.

Chichester Hospital's mortuary where Cdr Crabb's body was taken after its discovery.

Chichester Police Station where Cdr Crabb's items of clothing were held.

What breathing apparatus did Cdr Crabb use?

The evidence as to which oxygen breathing set Cdr Crabb used is conflicting.

The breathing apparatus described by fisherman Harry Cole when the body was discovered the first time, did not resemble anything that was in current use, either in the UK or Italy. If his assertions that the set had two breathing tubes and a slab lead weight were correct, then it did however have similarities with an oxygen set known as the Under Water Swimming Breathing Apparatus (UWSBA) produced by Dunlop and designed for British frogmen for special operations during WW2, only nine years previously at the time. These were operations associated with clearing underwater obstacles on the beaches in preparation for D-Day. The set incorporated a breathing bag that went around the back of the neck, twin breathing hoses that went over each shoulder and slab lead weights at the front.

The UWSBAs had only become obsolete two years previously in 1954 so the diving stores at *Vernon* would very likely have held a large number of returned sets. The set incorporated two oxygen cylinders with a total capacity of 4 cubic feet (113 litres). Assuming an average oxygen consumption of 1.5 litres per minute, the oxygen would have lasted for 75 minutes. The oxygen supply to the counterlung was achieved by manually turning a valve on an as-required basis. It had a 4 lb charge of Protosorb carbon dioxide absorbent with an estimated endurance of 3 hours maximum.

The contemporary RN oxygen set (Pattern 5562 "Shallow Water Breathing Apparatus" – SWBA) which was introduced in 1953 used a single breathing hose, the lead weights were small, ball-shaped in a pouch on the back and the breathing bag (counterlung) did not go around the back of the neck. The set carried two oxygen cylinders

Underwater Swimmer's Breathing Apparatus (UWSBA).
An oxygen rebreather used for covert operations during WW2. It had become obsolete two
years prior to Cdr Crabb's diving operation. Note the distinctive pattern of the swim fins
and the urinal port in the dry suit.

The navy's Pattern 5562 Shallow Water Breathing Apparatus.
This was the oxygen rebreather in use by the RN Shallow Water Divers at the time of
Cdr Crabb's diving operations. The illustration shows the set rigged for swimming. In this
configuration, there was no oxygen reducer and the diver operated a manual valve on his left
side to inflate the counterlung as required. This gave the set an endurance of up to 2 hours.

with a total capacity of 147.6 litres, for normal operation and an extra, emergency cylinder with a further 73.8 litres of oxygen. The Protosorb carbon dioxide absorbent canister carried a 2 lb charge of Protosorb. The SWBA Pattern 5562 could be rigged in one of two modes: Shallow Diving or Swimming. In the latter mode the oxygen supply was controlled manually and it was stated at the time of its introduction to have a maximum endurance of two hours.

The sketch of the equipment recovered from the body by Harry Cole (page 57), though crude and inaccurate, more closely resembles a SWBA Pattern 5562 than a UWSBA.

Furthermore, in view of Lt Cdr Franklin's statement that the breathing set used by Cdr Crabb had a maximum endurance of two hours, it is the author's opinion that on the balance of probabilities the set used was the SWBA Pattern 5562 rigged for swimming. This would be consistent with the fact that Cdr Crabb was diving from HMS *Maidstone's* own launch which was itself a diving school for Shallow Water Divers headed up by A Lewis and would therefore have had a ready supply of these breathing sets and, importantly, the means to charge them with oxygen.

Was it Cdr Crabb's body?

On 10 June 1957 the Chief Pathologist at St Richards Hospital, Chichester, Dr Donald Plimsoll King carried out the Post Mortem examination of the body.

He concluded that the body could have been in the water for at least six months and could well have been in the water for at least fourteen months. His description included:

"Above the waist, parts of the body, including the skull, had disappeared although certain bones, including the left humerus and both scapulae, remained. The abdominal cavity was empty except below the waist-band of

Dr Donald Plimsoll King the Chief Pathologist at St Richard's Hospital, Chichester. He carried out the post mortem examination on Cdr Crabb's body.

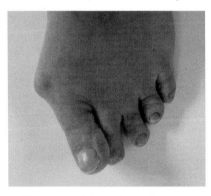

Illustration of the condition known as hallux valgus. Note the bunion and the inward deflection of the big toe.
This is not Cdr Crabb's body and is used for illustrative purposes only.

the suit. The organs had undergone extensive post mortem change including a change known as adipocere, but they were recognisable … He also found there was a condition called valgus which was a condition of the toes in which the big toe, which was the hallux, was turned outwards. The joint of the big toe was enlarged and disjointed. With regard to the hair on the body the pubic hair was intact and the colour was clearly a light brown and in certain lights when dry it had a gingerish tinge. The legs were in a good state of preservation and he would describe them as muscular and well formed and, apart from the feet, there was no deformity. They were quite straight.

From the adipocere, he concluded that the body had been in the water for at least six months and could well have been in the water for at least 14 months.

On the 14th June 1957, he went to the Mortuary and examined the remains again. He looked at the left knee and saw a scar.

His report also included the following details:

- *Length of feet 8.74 inches (22.2 cm)*
- *Moderate degree of bilateral hallux valgus* [also referred to as a 'bunion']
- *He was circumcised*
- *Small man, about 5ft 6ins*

The subsequent attempts at identification of the body produced conflicting accounts.

Cdr Crabb's former wife, Margaret Elaine Crabb viewed the body at Bognor Mortuary on 11 June 1957. She could not identify the feet as those of Cdr Crabb although she was not able to say definitely that they were not his feet. She described him as a short man, not as tall as she, her height being 5′5″. His legs were very straight and muscular and the hair on his body was very light brown inclined to ginger.

The body was viewed by Lt William McLanachan at 16.00 hours the same day. Lt McLanachan stated he "cannot definitely identify the body as that of Commander Crabb" but *"that the feet are similar inasmuch that they are small and appear to be slightly splayed."*

Cdr Gutteridge has stated:

It was a little surprising that McLanachan, who did not know Crabb well, was chosen for this unpleasant task whereas I, who lived in Chichester, was serving at the Underwater Countermeasures & Weapons Establishment where Crabb last served and probably knew Crabb in his later life better than anyone except his wife, was not asked to be involved in any identification … for which I was most grateful.

Petty Officer Ron McKinley CGM viewed the body and agreed it was that of Cdr Crabb.

Sydney Knowles was adamant that it was not the body of Cdr Crabb. He claimed he was shown the body and he was told by the Chief Inspector of Police:

"We know this is not the body of Commander Crabb but I want you to say it is the body of Commander Crabb"

But Knowles' description of the body differs from the others. In his book *A Diver in the Dark* he claims that when he saw it, it was still wearing the rubber dry suit though it had been cut open to display the body. Surprisingly, he described the suit as the type used by the navy which was a one-piece suit fitted with an urinal port. He also described the remains of a heavy duty submariner's sweater. This all conflicts with the evidence given by Franklin, McLanachan as well as Eric Blake and Ron Collins of C E Heinke & Co Ltd above and that of the other clothing described below. In my view Knowles' version is unfortunately unreliable.

Knowles was shown a photograph of the feet of Cdr Crabb but *"He was not able to say from the photographs shown to him whether the feet are those of Crabb."*

If Knowles was shown a photograph of Cdr Crabb's feet, why would he not have been able to undertake the same exercise when he allegedly saw the actual body. This throws further doubt on Knowles's claim that he actually saw the body. Knowles confirmed that Cdr Crabb had strong legs with large calves due to all the swimming he did. He described how Cdr Crabb had sustained an inverted "Y" scar on the side of his left knee. He said he looked closely for two scars he knew of on Cdr Crabb's legs but found none. This conflicts with the evidence of a piece of skin taken from the corpse which was alleged to bear such a scar. He added that Cdr Crabb used a two-piece dry suit with a neck seal instead of a hood. He used to wear maroon swimming shorts and two sets of combination underwear to wear alternately, one khaki in colour and the other blue. He also used blue socks.

Lt McLanachan viewed the diving equipment at Chichester Police Station on 11 June 1957. It included:

1 Frogman's two piece suit, in good condition but with marine growth, marked HEINKE LONDON inside waist band; soles similarly marked 9-10; two piece; inside of left leg and at feet large areas of rust

1 pair swim fins similar to RN pattern (marked Pattern 3386)[6]
2 sorbo pads
1 pair Maroon bathing trunks; "Just men"
1 pair nylon socks; St Michael brand, size 10-12
1 pair blue stockinette combinations (top half missing 18"zip)
1 pair nylon combinations, top torn
1 piece of undervest

Eric James Blake, Managing Director of C E Heinke & Co Ltd identified the two-piece suit with neck seal which he said was the type that had been sold to Cdr Crabb on 11 October 1955. He said Cdr Crabb always expressed a preference for a suit with neck seal rather than one with a hood attached.

Ron Chamberlain of Siebe Gorman & Co Ltd has referred to his friend Ron Collins, a manager at C E Heinke who stated that the suit found on the body:

"... was a Heinke Dry Suit and quoted the Number inside ... confirmed that that Numbered Suit was supplied to Buster Crabb."

This conflicts with the statement of Eric Blake. If the suit had been numbered, then this information should have been provided by Blake at the Inquest. I have not seen any official reference to such a number having been observed.

Detective Superintendent Allan Hoare described "marks of rust" around the legs making it "apparent that the body had been held by being caught on an underwater metal object". Lt Cdr Franklin, having seen the clothing found on the body has stated:

"It appears to me to be similar to the clothing which Crabb was wearing when I assisted him over the side of the boat and in my own mind I am convinced that it is the same clothing."

Newspaper reports suggested:

---

[6] "Pattern 3386" is the Admiralty Pattern number for the fins so they actually were naval fins and not only "similar to RN pattern".

"There was a strong suspicion amongst some defence chiefs that the body had not been in the water 14 months.

Pat Rose, Cdr Crabb's fiancée at the time of his disappearance, never accepted that Cdr Crabb had died during the dive or that the body recovered was that of Cdr Crabb.

Cdr Crabb's mother was not convinced it was his body.

The Coroner eventually concluded he was satisfied the body was that of Cdr Crabb.

After this formal declaration, if it was not the body of Cdr Crabb and he had indeed ended up in Russia, then the Russians had a first class opportunity for a propaganda coup by parading Cdr Crabb for all the world to see. The fact that this did not happen supports the view that it was the body of Cdr Crabb.

On the other hand, the fact that the body recovered from Chichester harbour was almost certainly planted there by a security agency, it did provide the opportunity to plant a replacement body. Furthermore, it was not entirely outside the capability of a security agency to produce a suitably decomposed and similar replacement body.

However, in the author's opinion, based on the above evidence, though it is conflicting and far from conclusive, on the balance of probabilities the body was that of Cdr Crabb.

The Inquest

The Inquest, held in camera (ie, not open to the public) at the Court House, Chichester, was opened on 11 June 1957. It lasted for two minutes. The Coroner's officer, PC Dennis Castleden simply accounted for the clothing found on the body and the Coroner, George Frederick Leslie Bridgman adjourned the proceedings for two weeks. It was reopened on 26 June 1957 at 15.00 hours without any jury and lasted for less than one hour.

Witness statements included those of:

- Dr Donald Plimsoll King, the pathologist who conducted the autopsy
- John Seymour Randall, one of the fishermen who found the body
- Police Constable Ronald George Williams, who attended at the recovery of the body
- George William Bontock, a civil servant who kept records of RNVR (Royal Naval Volunteer Reserve) officers.
- Miss Amy Frances Thomas, the manageress of Cdr Crabb's flat in Hans Road, London
- Mrs Margaret Elaine Crabb, Cdr Crabb's former wife.
- Eric James Blake, a director of Heinke & Co Ltd who made Cdr Crabb's diving suit
- Sydney James Knowles, Cdr Crabb's former diving colleague
- Colin Grey Turner, a shoe specialist

The Court House at Chichester where the Inquest on Cdr Crabb was held.

- Detective Superintendent Allan Hoare, who had been in charge of enquiries concerning the body

It appears that the Admiralty was successful in preventing Franklin, who was the last person to see Cdr Crabb alive, from being called as a witness and no reference was made to him by the Coroner in his conclusions. Indeed, not a single representative from the Royal Navy or MI6 was called to give evidence.

A note from the Head of Naval Law to Chief of Naval Intelligence prior to the Inquest suggests it was effectively choreographed:

"The body will be identified by the evidence of the following:
a)   Crabb's wife …
b)   Heinke's …
c)   A man in Newcastle …
The Coroner is aware of the background to the case and is not asking for the appearance of any embarrassing naval witness …
The answer to all questions continues to be that we have nothing to add to what the Prime Minister said in the House of Commons in May 1956 …"

Rear Admiral J G T Inglis, Director of Naval Intelligence has stated that The Coroner and Chief Constable were *"being most co-operative"*. A government document stated that *"The Home Office think they would be able to persuade him* [the Coroner] *to avoid awkward questions."*

The Coroner subsequently returned an open verdict on the cause of death and said he was satisfied that the remains were those of Cdr Crabb. There was no evidence of the cause of death.

The Funeral

A Requiem Mass was celebrated in Portsmouth Roman Catholic Cathedral for Cdr Crabb at noon on Friday, 5 July 1957. It was organised by Mr James Gleeson, author of *The Frogmen* on behalf of Cdr Crabb's mother and paid for by the Admiralty. But such was the Admiralty's sensitivity, there were no naval honours. Attendance by serving personnel was to be unofficial and out of uniform. About

Lt Cdr Harry Wardle, one of the bearers of Cdr Crabb's coffin.

eighty people attended who were mainly women. The six bearers of the coffin, all in civilian clothes, included Lt Cdr Bill Filer MBE GM, Lt Cdr Bill McLanachan MBE BEM, Lt Barry Barrington MBE and Lt Cdr Harry Wardle.

The family mourners were headed by Cdr Crabb's mother, Mrs Beatrice Crabb who was small and frail. Cdr Crabb's former wife 43-year-old Mrs Margaret Crabb did not attend.

Cdr Crabb's coffin was draped in a Union Jack. On top lay his sword stick along with a card bearing a French inscription taken from Joan of Arc's sword in Rheims Cathedral. Roughly translated it said *"I was there at the fight, so I will be there at the glory"*.

Following Mass, Cdr Crabb's body was interred at Milton Cemetery, Portsmouth at noon. The entire cemetery was closed to the public for the duration of the burial ceremony. When the author went to view the grave in March 2013, he was informed that about half a dozen people a year visited the grave.

Cdr Crabb's grave at Milton Cemetery, Portsmouth.

Subsequent events

The bungled cover-up including the misunderstandings between the Admiralty/Naval Intelligence and the Foreign Office/MI6 before, during and after Cdr Crabb's fatal dive is a story in its own right but it is not considered here. Suffice it to say that the Prime Minister, Sir Anthony Eden was highly displeased and there was a major shake-up. Many 'heads rolled', to a large extent discretely. The Prime Minister's displeasure would of course have been incurred by the Naval Intelligence diving operation as well as the MI6/Crabb operation, since both went ahead against his directive and without his knowledge. However, it seems that MI6/SIS bore the main brunt of the Prime Minister's wrath.

Sir Anthony Eden released a statement on 14 May stating:

It would not be in the public interest to disclose the circumstances in which Commander Crabb is presumed to have met his death. I think it necessary, in the special circumstances of this case, to make it clear that what was done was done without the authority or the knowledge of Her Majesty's Ministers. Appropriate disciplinary steps are being taken.

Sir Anthony had commissioned an immediate in-house investigation into the affair on 9 May to be conducted personally by the Head of the Civil Service, Sir Edward Bridges. He was instructed to investigate the Cdr Crabb intelligence operation. There was no mention of the Royal Navy/Naval Intelligence operation. The detailed report was on the Prime Minister's desk by 18 May.

The Prime Minister approved the disciplinary measures to be taken against individuals in the Admiralty and Foreign Office in the light of the Bridges Enquiry. They were co-ordinated to be taken on Wednesday, 27 June 1956.

The Rt Hon Viscount 'Jim' Cilcennin, First Lord of the Admiralty, resigned on 1 September 1956. He had proposed this action to the Prime Minister on 13 May 1956 as a means of minimising the embarrassment to the government.

Major General Sir John Sinclair, Chief of MI6 'retired' and was relieved by MI5's Sir Dick White in 1956. Several other senior members of MI6 closely associated with Sinclair also 'retired' around the same time.

Sir Ivone Kirkpatrick, Permanent Secretary, Foreign Office was also told he had been guilty of an error of judgement in not keeping his Minister informed. He retired in February 1957.

Rear Admiral John G T Inglis OBE, Director of Naval Intelligence, was censured, but he kept his job until he retired in 1960. He became a Vice-Admiral in 1958.

Sir John Lang GCB, Permanent Secretary of the Admiralty was told he had been guilty of an error of judgement in not keeping his Minister informed. But he kept his job and remained a prominently successful civil servant until his retirement in 1961.

Lt Cdr Joe Brooks' career advanced no further. It was not helped when he accidentally blew both his legs off in an attempt to dispose of a whale shark which was interfering with some diving trials off Falmouth later the same year. He miraculously survived the incident though two civilians in the same boat were killed outright. He was invalided out of the Navy in April 1959. He went on to a very successful career running a commercial diving company based at Havant (Mobell Marine Ltd).

Nicholas Elliott in MI6 appears to have escaped censure and remained until his retirement around 1968.

Lord Louis Mountbatten, who was out of the country throughout the affair, claimed he knew nothing of Cdr Crabb's mission. He claimed to have instructed his Vice Chief of Naval Staff, Vice-Admiral Sir William Davis that no such operation should be undertaken. Sir William Davis denied ever receiving the instruction.

Two years after Cdr Crabb's disappearance, Lt Cdr Joe Brooks (now on prosthetic legs) was in Malta advising on the filming of "The Silent Enemy", the well-known film re-enacting Cdr Crabb's epic dives at Gibraltar during WW2.

The next time a Soviet cruiser visited Portsmouth Harbour on a goodwill visit in 1976, it was the turn of the *Obrakzovy*. On the bridge was Lt Cdr Cyril Lafferty RN who was acting as a liaison officer with the cruiser's captain. As the cruiser edged its way through the narrow entrance in to the harbour, the Soviet Navigation Officer nudged Lt Cdr Lafferty and pointed out of the window to starboard, to 'The Point' at Old Portsmouth where the Still and West public house stands. He then pointed to the equivalent location on their navigation chart and read out the Russian text. Lt Cdr Lafferty explained he couldn't speak Russian, so the Navigation Officer translated it for him:

"It reads: Crabb Point".

PART 3

Conclusions

Cause of death

On the balance of probabilities, it is most likely that Cdr Crabb died during his dive. Only this possibility is considered here. It is most likely he died shortly after briefly surfacing when he was observed by three of the Soviet sailors at around 07.30 hours. My own enquiries to a reliable and senior Russian source returned their official opinion that Cdr Crabb probably drowned whilst investigating the hull of the *Ordzhonikidze*.

The cause of his death could have been due to any of several individual reasons or any combination of them, probably aggravated by cold, including:

- Oxygen poisoning
- Carbon dioxide poisoning
- Heart attack
- Drowning
- Exhaustion

It is unlikely to have been due to lack of oxygen as he had only been underwater for only 30 minutes.

Body movement

It is most likely his body would have been negatively buoyant and even more so if his counterlung had flooded.

Lt Cdr Franklin has stated:

"The weight and nature of the [breathing] *apparatus were such that if, through mal-adjustment subsequent to entering the water or through some physical failure on the part of the wearer, he becomes unconscious,*

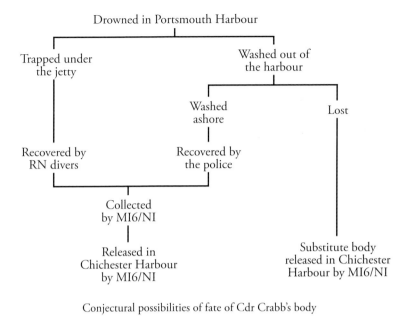

Conjectural possibilities of fate of Cdr Crabb's body

---

it is most unlikely that the body would rise to the surface so long as the apparatus remains in place."

Two possibilities exist as to what would have then happened to his body. It was either:

a) carried by a tidal eddy under the piled structure of the jetty and there became entangled in debris or

b) washed out of the harbour by the ebbing tide.

a) TRAPPED UNDER SOUTH RAILWAY JETTY

It is known that under that particular jetty the sea bed was strewn with all kinds of debris including coils of steel cable that could snag and entrap a diver. An Admiralty diver has stated that there were large coils of rusting steel cable up against the quay wall, possibly scrap cable placed there to minimise any scouring by eddies from ships' propellers, or simply just dumped.

It would have been logical and expected that the authorities would have wanted to check whether Crabb's body had ended up under the jetty.

An Admiralty note dated 25.05.56 suggesting where Crabb's body may have ended up states:

"There is practically no silt on the dredged berth and the bottom is hard clay. The underside of the jetty is encumbered with wire ropes and other debris. The tidal stream on ebb and flow sets in towards the jetty and there are local eddies which maintain northward flow after high water …

Diving Inspection – very laborious owing to debris. A quick look along the front of the jetty could be done in 5 days (1 week) probably at a cost of about £60. A proper inspection of the whole of the space under the jetty would take 3 or 4 weeks or perhaps even more at £50/60 a week.

If anything is there I would personally think its most probable location is caught up in the debris near the front of the jetty."

An official note observed:

"An inspection of the space under the jetty would be a dangerous operation because of obstructions, wire ropes, old anchors etc."

The late Surgeon Vice Admiral Sir John Rawlins has stated that he was on a diving course at HMS *Vernon* shortly after Crabb's disappearance. One of the exercises he was required to undertake whilst on course was to assist in a search for "anything interesting" under the same jetty. Even if any trainee divers failed to find a body, it would have been reasonable to order a thorough search by qualified Clearance Divers in due course. If Crabb's body had ended up under the jetty, then it is almost certain it would have been recovered by naval divers. In my opinion, this is the most likely turn of events.

If the body was found, it would not have been in the interest of the navy or the government to release the information where and when it was found. Indeed on 14 May 1956 the Chief Constable of the crime office in Chichester wrote to all local police authorities in Portsmouth area warning them that should Crabb's body surface:

"It is absolutely essential that the finding of the body is not to be disclosed to the press."

The authorities clearly wanted to be able to control the eventual disclosure of the reappearance of the body and under circumstances that best suited them.

b) WASHED OUT OF THE HARBOUR

If the body had been washed out of the harbour, then it appears it would have disappeared into the English Channel. A report dated 5 June 2014, by a forensic hydrographic expert in the tidal drift of bodies, Mr Matthew French, CMarTech, FCInstCES, FIMarEST, FRGS, MRIN, has concluded:

- *It is most unlikely that the body would have left the main channel out of Portsmouth Harbour once it was in the water until it reached the two forts [Horse Sand and No Man's Land].*

- *It is most unlikely, if not impossible, for a negatively buoyant body exiting Portsmouth Harbour to leave the channel between Southsea castle and the forts and then travel eastwards and on into Chichester Harbour.*

- *In my opinion, assuming that the body exited Portsmouth Harbour, it was carried by the tidal stream past the two forts and into the English Channel. From there, it could not have entered Chichester Harbour.*

The inescapable conclusion is that the body recovered from Chichester Harbour did not arrive there by natural means. Which begs the question "Who put it there?"

Chichester Harbour

On the balance of probabilities, the body recovered from Chichester Harbour was that of Cdr Crabb. But how did it get there?

Why, of all the police forces, should the Chichester police in Sussex on 14 May 1956 get involved by sending out the order not to disclose the finding of a body? It is a strange coincidence that the body was eventually discovered in the jurisdiction of the Chichester police force and where the Chief Constable and Coroner were, according to MI6, "most co-operative".

Is it possible that the decision had already been taken to release the body in Chichester Harbour in due course if or when it was found, if indeed it had not already been found? Had the body been found four or five days earlier when the dredging activities were observed along the South Railway Jetty?

In the author's opinion the most likely explanation is that the re-appearance of Crabb's body in Chichester harbour was not due to any tidal drift but rather more likely to have been orchestrated by one of the security agencies, MI6 or Naval Intelligence. The body was placed in one of the heavily-fished tidal creeks in Chichester Harbour with the intention that it would, at some time thereafter be netted, dredged up or washed ashore.

A possible scenario that could fit the above supposition would be that the Royal Navy conducted a search for Cdr Crabb's body under South Railway Jetty sometime after the Soviet ships had left. It would certainly have been a logical action to take. Dredging activities were carried out north and south of King's Stairs on 10 May, following Cdr Crabb's disappearance undoubtedly in an attempt to find his body. If Cdr Crabb's body had been recovered either by naval divers or dredging activities, the security agencies would not have been in a hurry to declare their find. It would not have suited them at the time to reveal either that they had found it or where they had found it. The best solution would have been to 'store' the body in a secure sea water location (to ensure its normal decomposition as would be expected during a prolonged immersion) and then quietly release the body in Chichester Harbour, a respectable time after the departure of the Soviet warships and after the press feeding frenzy had died down.

But where could MI6 find a suitable secure location to store the body?

It was perhaps fortuitous that MI6's premier field operations training centre was based in Fort Monckton, today called No1 Military Training Establishment, just two miles away, on the sea front in Gosport. Indeed his body was reported to have been seen there a short while after his disappearance. This confirms that the body had been recovered and later placed in Chichester harbour.

Fort Monckton at Gosport. The MI6 training centre.

It would also help to explain the conflicting information concerning the breathing apparatus used. Namely, Franklin's version indicated the use of the very latest oxygen equipment being used by the RN Clearance Divers (single hose) and the fisherman's version which referred to a twin hose set. If Cdr Crabb's body was eventually found wearing the latest Royal Navy breathing equipment, it would suggest the direct involvement of the RN in his covert operation. So the opportunity was taken to substitute an obsolete, twin hose breathing apparatus, which would weaken any attempted link to the RN.

This all goes to reveal the extraordinary lengths to which the intelligence agencies went to, to mislead and provide more significant reasons why the embargo on the documentation has been extended to 100 years.

But why would anyone want to produce Cdr Crabb's, or even a fake body in the first place?

The answer lies in a report dated 29 May 1956, when the Admiralty stated that "*Two problems remain to be dealt with*". The most important of these was "*the establishment of or presumption of death.*"

The appearance of Cdr Crabb's body would tie up this embarrassing loose end, simplify the proceedings and allow the books to be closed.

Or so they hoped.

APPENDICES

Appendix 1

The Admiralty Underwater Countermeasures and Weapons Establishment originated in the Mining Department formed in the Admiralty in 1915. In 1919 it became the Mine Design Department at HMS *Vernon*, where it remained until 1939. The Department was dispersed during the Second World War, and reconstituted in 1946 as the Admiralty Mining Establishment at Leigh Park, Havant. It undertook research into the design, location and neutralisation of mines, and into torpedoes and other underwater weapons.

The main administrative headquarters were based in Leigh Park House whilst the research departments, including the diving group, were based at West Leigh House about a mile away.

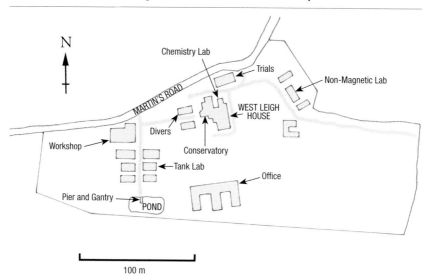

Plan of Underwater Countermeasures and Weapons Establishment (UCWE). The area is now a housing estate. The pond was used for trials of underwater equipment.

In 1951 it became the Admiralty Underwater Countermeasures and Weapons Establishment. Gordon Gutteridge was put in charge of staff requirements of a small specialist group for the development of mine investigation equipment and the relevant diving equipment "platform" to use it. Then to co-ordinate the effort and set up a top-of-the-line Experimental Diving Trials Team attached to UCWE, the Admiralty put Crabb in charge as Diving Officer with rank of Cdr RNVR with a 2-year contract. UCWE closed in 1959 when underwater research was moved to the Admiralty Underwater Weapons Establishment (AUWE) at Portland. Some key personnel including Ray Common moved to the Admiralty Experimental Diving Unit (AEDU) at HMS *Vernon*.

Mr Winstock had a staff of about 20 which included Margaret Johnson (who worked there from spring 1951 to March 1954) and Clem Hoagan. They were involved with high speed photography of torpedoes. Crabb used to take Margaret Johnson with him on his official trips to Farnborough and Portsmouth. She said she was impressed by him but was a little scared of him. Another of his associates at UCWE was John Lintorn, who described Cdr Crabb as a gentleman in every respect.

Appendix 2

MAITLAND PENDOCK

Cdr Crabb worked part-time for Pendock selling antique furniture. They had been close friends for a long time.

London Gazette, 18 October, 1949

PENDOCK. Harold Victor Maitland, lately residing at 41, Bramham Gardens, London, S.W.5, but now of no fixed address, carrying on business under the style of Hayes (Marshall Interior Decoration Course, and lately carrying on business at 69, Fleet Street, London, E.C.4, as a BUSINESS CONSULTANT, described in the Receiving Order as Harold Victor Maitland Pendock, sued as Maitland Pendock, formerly of 52, Kings Court North, Kings Road, Chelsea, S.W.3, and lately of Blayden Manor, Buckdown, in the county of Devon, but whose present address the Petitioners have been unable to ascertain but who is a domiciled Englishman, domiciled in England, and whose occupation is unknown. Court—HIGH COURT OF JUSTICE. No. of Matter—349 of 1949. Date of Order—Oct. 10, 1949. Date of Filing Petition- July 1, 1949.

Frogman Spy, by M G & J A Welham, 1990

[Maitland] *owned a company called Elmbourne Ltd, with its office in Seymour Place, London … an advertising consultant, jolly, middle aged with round Pickwickian face; … sold build-it-yourself furniture … associated with Anthony Blunt, Burgess, Maclean and Philby; pp23-24. The Welhams also mentioned that Pendock was questioned and beaten up by MI5 officers as a suspected communist sympathiser; pp74-75.*

John McCormick Recollections

http://www.scribd.com/doc/18647595/4/

After Crabb disappeared in Portsmouth, Maitland began to ask questions in high places about Crabb. He was told to drop the subject. When the body of a frogman was found and buried in 1957, he was taken and interrogated by MI5. There followed further interrogations and intimidation and in 1958, Maitland, my grandmother Helen and dad went on 'holiday' to a very remote location in Southern Ireland. It was strange because they were going to camp and the family did not do camping. During the trip, Maitland was "irritable" and was taken to a small cottage Hospital for a check-up. Granny was told to go away and come back later that day. Returning to the Hospital to check on how Maitland was, she was informed that her husband had died. She never saw the body. There was no release form for the body; there is no evidence of an undertaker being involved and nor was there was an autopsy. None of the family actually saw the body of Maitland. There was a funeral, but granny always maintained that it was not Maitland in the coffin. At the time granny instructed the family that they were not to mention Maitland's name again.

Appendix 3

ADMIRALTY EXPERIMENTAL DIVING UNIT (AEDU)

This Unit was based within HMS *Vernon*. Its premises moved around Vernon over the years. In 1956 it was based in a building near the "Mining Tank".

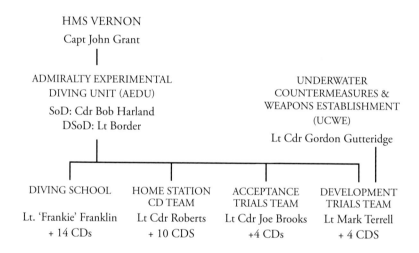

Appendix 4

HMS *Deepwater* and Diving School

Senior Clearance Diving Officer	Lt Cdr George Albert Franklin
Instructor	Lt F J D Kelly
Instructor	Lt Taylor
Instructor	Lt K C Lewis

HMS *Deepwater* onboard which was located the RN Diving School.

Appendix 5

HMS *MAIDSTONE*

HMS *Maidstone* was a submarine support ship, 8.900 tons, launched in 1937. In 1956 she was the mother ship to the 2nd and 7th Submarine Flotillas based at Portland. In 1956 she was also briefly the Flagship of the Commander-in-Chief of the Home Fleet at Portsmouth. Shallow Water Diving courses were conducted onboard in close association with the Diving School on HMS *Deepwater* at HMS *Vernon*. These courses were specifically in the use of oxygen rebreathing equipment. There would therefore have been a very close relationship between the head of the Deepwater Diving School (Lt Cdr Franklin) and the officer in charge of the training onboard Maidstone (A Lewis). The use of Maidstone's launch by Lt Cdr Franklin and Cdr Crabb for the diving operation would therefore appear logical.

HMS *Maidstone*

Appendix 6

Service Record
Commander (Sp) L K P Crabb RNVR

TEMPORARY SUB LIEUTENANT (SP)

KING ALFRED	07.08.41 - 21.08.41
WASP	22.08.41 - 06.11.41

TEMPORARY LIEUTENANT (SP)

WASP	07.11.41 – 25.11.41
PRESIDENT addl for duty outside Admiralty with DUBD	26.11.41 – 26.10.42
CORMORANT addl as BSO Gibraltar	27.10.42 – 28.12.43
CORMORANT addl (Special Service)	29.12.43 – 30.03.44

TEMPORARY ACTING LIEUTENANT-COMMANDER (SP)

CORMORANT addl (Special Service)	31.03.44 – ?
BYRSA addl for BS and RMS duties on staff of FOWIT	? – 22.06.44
BYRSA addl as RMS and BSO Party "Jip"	23.06.44 – 11.09.44
BYRSA addl for MBDU No1 i/c	12.09.44 – 23.12.44
BYRSA addl (sick)	24.12.44 – ?
FABIUS addl for duty with NP 'C'	? – ?
ST ANGELO addl	? – ?
VICTORY (not to join)	17.02.47 – 11.05.47

VERNON addl for SWD
  Refresher course   12.05.47 – 22.05.47
VICTORY (not to join)   23.05.47 – 25.05.47
STAGG addl in charge of
  'P' parties, Haifa   26.05.47 – 14.12.47
VERNON   15.12.47 – 29.04.48

RELEASED CLASS A 30.04.48

LIEUTENANT-COMMANDER (SP)
VERNON for RECLAIM addl   121 days training

Recalled for 18 months (but stayed 3½ years!); service as follows:

LIEUTENANT-COMMANDER (SP)
VERNON addl for duty with
  CUCWE for clearance diving   12.10.51 – 29.06.52

COMMANDER (SP)
VERNON addl for duty with
  CUCWE for clearance diving   30.06.52 – 07.04.55

RELEASED   08.04.55

PRESIDENT (RNVR) LIST II   08.04.55–   DATE

DECORATIONS:
George Medal   (AFO 518/44)
OBE   (AFO 7319/45)

Appendix 7

Books dedicated to the Cdr Crabb case

1956: *Commander Crabb*
       by Marshall Pugh, Macmillan & Co Ltd

1960: *Frogman Extraordinary*
       by J Bernard Hutton, Neville Spearman Ltd
       Frogman Spy, in the USA

1968: *Commander Crabb is Alive*
       by J Bernard Hutton, Library 33 Ltd

1970: *The Fake Defector*
       by J Bernard Hutton, Howard Baker Publishers Ltd, SBN 09
       307060 8

1990: *Frogman Spy*
       by MG and JA Welham, W H Allen & Co plc, ISBN
       1-85227-138-8

2007: *The Final Dive*
       by Don Hale, Sutton Publishing, ISBN 978-0-7509-4574-5

2010: *The Crabb Enigma*
       by Mike and Jacqui Welham, Troubador Publishing Ltd,
       ISBN 978 1848763 821

Index